SECRET
LEITH

Jack Gillon

AMBERLEY

First published 2019

Amberley Publishing
The Hill, Stroud
Gloucestershire, GL5 4EP

www.amberley-books.com

Copyright © Jack Gillon, 2019

The right of Jack Gillon to be identified as the
Author of this work has been asserted in accordance
with the Copyrights, Designs and Patents Act 1988.

ISBN 978 1 4456 8609 7 (print)
ISBN 978 1 4456 8610 3 (ebook)

British Library Cataloguing in Publication Data.
A catalogue record for this book is available from the
British Library.

Origination by Amberley Publishing.
Printed in Great Britain.

Contents

Introduction

Leith is a quaint old-fashioned looking burgh, full of crooked alleys, and rambling narrow wynds, scattered about in the most irregular and lawless fashion. (*Memorials of Edinburgh in the Olden Time,* Daniel Wilson, 1848)

Leith was first established on the banks of the Water of Leith, at the point where the river entered the Firth of Forth. The first historical reference to the town dates from 1140, when the harbour and fishing rights were granted to Holyrood Abbey by David I. The early settlement was centred on the area bounded by the Shore, Water Street, Tolbooth Wynd and Broad Wynd. Leith became Edinburgh's port in 1329, when Robert I granted control of the shoreline hamlet to the burgh of Edinburgh. In the early days it consisted of the two independent settlements of South Leith and North Leith.

Leith frequently features in the power struggles that took place in Scotland, and the battles, landings and sieges of Leith have had an influence on its development. It was attacked by the Earl of Hertford in 1544 during the Rough Wooing – his mission was to arrange a marriage between the young Mary, Queen of Scots and her English cousin, later Edward VI. Three years later, Leith was pillaged after the defeat of the Scottish army at the Battle of Pinkie. Immediately following this, Mary of Guise, the

Leith from the Firth of Forth, 1820.

Roman Catholic Regent of Scotland, moved the seat of government to Leith and the town was fortified.

Leith expanded significantly during the nineteenth century, associated with railway building and the growth of the docks. Port-related industries and warehousing also grew rapidly during this period. This contemporary description paints a vivid portrait of the port at the time: 'Leith possesses many productive establishments, such as ship-building and sail-cloth manufactories, manufactories of glass, a corn-mill, many warehouses for wines and spirits, and there are also other manufacturing establishments besides those for the making of cordage for brewing, distilling, and rectifying spirits, refining sugar, preserving tinned meats, soap and candle manufactories, with several extensive cooperages, iron-foundries, flourmills, tanneries and saw-mills.'

In 1833, Leith was established as an independent municipal and parliamentary burgh with full powers of local government. The town expanded as massive warehouses and additional docks were built: the Victoria Dock in 1851, the Albert Dock in 1881 and the Imperial Dock in 1903. After the passing of the Leith Improvement Act in 1880, many of the sixteenth- and seventeenth-century buildings were cleared away.

In 1920, despite a plebiscite in which the people of Leith voted 26,810 to 4,340 against the merger, Leith was incorporated into Edinburgh. However, Leith has always retained its own distinct identity and a passionate sense of individuality.

Many of the stories in this book have been told before by accomplished local historians. However, it is hoped that this book, by using early sources – media reports, contemporary with events, and a mix of old and new images – has uncovered some fresh aspects of the long and distinguished history of Leith, even for people that know it well.

A small part of lost Leith. An array of cigarette adverts on McLaggan's Newsagent shop at the corner of St Andrew Street and the Kirkgate.

1. Leith Walk and the Pilrig Muddles

Leith Walk at Pilrig.

Of all the streets in Edinburgh or Leith, the Walk, in former times, was certainly the street for boys and girls. From top to bottom, it was a scene of wonders and enjoyments peculiarly devoted to children. Besides the panoramas and caravan-shows, which were comparatively transient spectacles, there were several shows upon Leith Walk, which might be considered as regular fixtures. Who can forget the wax-works of Mrs Sands, which occupied a laigh shop opposite to the present Haddington Place, and at the door of which, besides various parrots, and sundry birds of Paradise, sat the wax figure of a little man in the dress of a French courtier of the ancient regime, reading one eternal copy of the Edinburgh Advertiser. The very outsides of these wonder-shops were an immense treat: all along the Walk, it was one delicious scene of squirrels hung out at doors, and monkeys dressed like soldiers and sailors. Even the half-penniless boy might here get his appetite for wonders to some extent gratified. (*Traditions of Edinburgh*, Robert Chambers, 1868)

The site of the Pilrig Muddle.

Coach passing the Halfway House.

The description of Leith Walk makes it sound like quite a cheerful place – although perhaps not so much for the squirrels. However, the history of Leith Walk has a much more grisly and darker side. The Gallow Lee, on the west side of the walk at Shrub Hill, was a site for the public execution of alleged witches, Covenanters and others that had been found guilty of major crimes. Some were left hanging in chains for years. The unfortunate victims were cremated on the spot – the ashes from centuries of executions were eventually carted away and converted into mortar for the construction of Edinburgh's New Town buildings.

DID YOU KNOW?
Leith Walk was the site of one of the early incarnations of the Botanical Gardens. It began as a physic garden in 1670, growing medicinal plants on a small site near Holyrood. By 1676, it occupied an area where the north-east corner of Waverley station now stands and was known as the Town Garden. In 1766, it moved to a 5-acre site in the grounds of what was the old Trinity Hospital on the Walk. Constantly outgrowing the various locations, the gardens finally moved to a new site on the east side of Inverleith House between 1823 and 1824. The gardener's cottage from the Leith Walk Botanical Gardens was moved to Inverleith in 2016.

Leith Walk originated from the defensive earthwork constructed in the mid-seventeenth century to defend the northern approach to Edinburgh against Oliver Cromwell's forces. It developed into a broad footpath for pedestrian use; hence the name Leith Walk. It was established as the main route between Edinburgh and Leith on completion of the North Bridge. In 1748, it was described as 'a very handsome gravel walk, twenty feet broad, which is kept in good repair at the public expense, and no horses suffered to come upon it.' After the North Bridge was completed in 1769, Leith Walk was opened to carriages and, by 1779, stagecoaches between Edinburgh and Leith were making 156 journeys a day.

Anderson's Leith stagecoach took an hour and a half to make the journey from Edinburgh's Tron Kirk to the Shore in Leith – surely it would have been faster on foot. It was described as a 'great lumbering affair drawn by a pair of ill-conditioned and ill-sized hacks, yoked to the carriage by old leathern straps and ropes, bearing evidence of many a mend.' After three quarters of an hour, it reached the Halfway House on Leith Walk where the carriage would frequently get stuck in a rut. The horses would slip their harness and assistance from patrons of the Halfway House would be required to extricate the carriage and reharness the horses. This was just the first of the Pilrig Muddles.

At the Edinburgh-Leith amalgamation inquiries in London a good deal was said about the tramway *Muddle* at Pilrig. I write to suggest, now that the amalgamation is assured, that the Tramway Committee of Edinburgh Town Council should meet without delay and consider whether it is not possible to reduce to some extent the discomforts of the *Muddle*. I have had occasion recently to travel a good deal to and from Leith by tramway, and some days the cable cars were stopped at a point which left passengers a walk of some 200 to 250 yards before they were able to join the Leith cars. (Letter to the *Scotsman*, 16 July 1920)

In 1905, when the newly created Leith Corporation Tramways pioneered the use of electric traction, an anomaly appeared that would take nearly twenty years and the unification of Edinburgh and Leith to sort out. Edinburgh's tram system was predominantly cable-run and Leith's, with its distinctive Munich Lake and ivory livery, was electrified. This meant that passengers travelling along Leith Walk were forced to change trams outside the Boundary Bar, and no doubt a few passengers resorted to the pub for a quick refreshment. It seems that Edinburgh favoured the cable system, as it was considered that the stanchions and overhead cables of an electric tram system would affect the architectural character of streets such as Princes Street. The merger of the two burghs in 1920 was the catalyst for the upgrading of the Edinburgh network to an electric system – Princes Street was converted from cable to electric operation overnight in October 1922. Electric trams finally crossed the frontier on 20 June 1923 and the chaotic interchange known as the *Pilrig Muddle* was finally eradicated.

As to the practical aspects of the case, the boundary line between Edinburgh and Leith was absolutely undistinguishable except on the map. The line passed through streets and even divided houses. It was actually the case that the head of a bed in a certain house was in Leith and the foot of the bed was in Edinburgh. There was in a certain public house a brass rod which was placed across the bar in order that any of the more questionable characters that came to drink there might know that, when they were on one side of the bar they were in Edinburgh, and when they were on the other side they were in Leith. (*Evidence Given to the Select Committee on the Edinburgh Amalgamation*, April 1896)

The confusion on the street was reflected in a nearby Leith Walk hostelry. The Boundary Bar on Leith Walk took its name from its location on the historic dividing line between Leith and Edinburgh. From 1833 to 1920, Leith was independent from Edinburgh and a municipal and parliamentary burgh with full powers of local government. Edinburgh and Leith had quite separate licensing laws during this time and the Boundary Bar, which straddled both burghs, adopted two sets of opening times. The Leith opening hours were more liberal and the bar had two separate entrances, one in Edinburgh and the other in Leith. Customers on the Edinburgh side were served until the official Edinburgh closing time and they could then move to the Leith side to enjoy a few more for the road. Police from the two separate burghs would also meet inside the bar to exchange prisoners. The Boundary Bar has gone through a number of name changes in recent years and it would be unfortunate if the name's link with Leith's past is lost.

2. Leith Central Station and the Prince of Wales in the Central Bar

Leith Central station.

The Italianate-style station building, with its corner clock tower at the foot of Leith Walk, was opened on 1 July 1903 by the North British Railway. The new station relieved Waverley of some of its suburban traffic and the seven-minute journey between Leith Central and Waverley, which cost one penny, was known as the Penny Jump. Leith Central station closed to passenger traffic on 7 April 1952, but continued to be used as a diesel maintenance depot until 1972, before its complete closure. The derelict station was said to have been much used by drug addicts and the inspiration for the ironic title of Irvine Welsh's book *Trainspotting*.

The railway company offered John Doig, the proprietor of an earlier pub known as the Central Bar at the junction of Leith Walk and Duke Street, larger premises in the new building. The bar was completed in 1899, a few years ahead of the station opening.

Tiled panel in the Central Bar depicting the Prince of Wales playing golf.

The Central was the station bar and a stair at the rear of the pub provided direct access to the station. This guaranteed a large number of patrons and no expense was spared in the fitting out of the interior. The bar has decorative relief tiling from the floor to the ceiling with inset panels showing sporting activities – yacht racing at Cowes Regatta, hare coursing and hunting with pointers. The panel depicting golf is represented by the then Prince of Wales, the future Edward VII (1841–1910), taking a fairway shot. The prince was a keen golfer and was appointed Captain of the St Andrew's Royal and Ancient course in 1863.

3. Julian the Tank Bank in Leith

Above: Julian, the Tank Bank.

Left: Tank Bank campaign advert.

It was during the breakfast hour that the tank rumbled into Leith. Much enthusiasm greeted its progress through the streets. Everywhere were large crowds who cheered lustily as the monster proceeded from the Caledonian Station in North Leith to the place allocated for it at the foot of Leith Walk. At the head of the procession came the band of the Royal Scots and a detachment of the same unit acted as military escort. Julian got a further cordial welcome when the time came for the opening ceremony. There was a gathering of several thousands when Provost Lindsay spoke of the high compliment that had been paid to Leith, in respect that it was the first town – apart from cities – that had received a visit from the tank. After the National Anthem had been sung, the crowd turned their attention to the counters. The first War Bond sold was purchased by a soldier who left later in the day for France. (*Daily Record and Mail*, 24 January 1918)

During the First World War, members of the public were encouraged to contribute to the war effort through National Savings. The Tank Bank Campaign was a unique and novel fundraising project which tempted the war-weary public to part with its hard-earned cash to help the war effort. It was the brainchild of the National War Savings Committee, which decided to capitalise on the public's interest in the new 'wonder weapon' and use tanks for the sale of war bonds and saving certificates.

Six Mark IV tanks were allocated to tour the towns and cities of Britain, in a campaign which raised many millions of pounds. In Scotland, tank 113, which was given the sobriquet *Julian*, visited the Scottish burghs at the beginning of 1918. In order to build excitement before the day of the tank's arrival, leaflets were dropped from a plane to advertise the event, then, on the scheduled day, the tank arrived with a great flourish and was put through its paces for the crowds in order to demonstrate its capabilities.

There were always concerns about the safety of the over-enthusiastic public who gathered to see *Julian*, as the tanks weren't easy to steer and the driver's vision was severely restricted. A police presence was required to maintain order in the crowd and a close escort of soldiers accompanied the tanks.

Julian arrived at the foot of Leith Walk on 23 January 1918 and was greeted by enthusiastic crowds. After speeches by local dignitaries, Julian's hatches were thrown open for deposits to be taken. On the first day Leithers and Leith companies had subscribed £367,410. Well over a million pounds was raised during the tank's four-day stay in Leith.

DID YOU KNOW?
In 1919, a number of old tanks were gifted to towns and cities in thanks for their financial help in the First World War. Edinburgh had one on display on Calton Hill and there was another on Leith Links. Due to a lack of funds, or general indifference at the time, they were scrapped in the 1920s, consigning this unique fundraising project to history.

4. The Kirkgate

The Kirkgate.

The principal street of Leith is the Kirkgate, a broad and somewhat stately thorough-fare, according to the prevalent proportions among the lanes and alleys of this close-packed little burgh. Time and modern taste have slowly, but very effectually, modified its antique features. No timber-fronted gable now thrusts its picturesque façade with careless grace beyond the line of more staid and formal-looking ashlar fronts. Even the crow-stepped gables of the sixteenth and seventeenth centuries are becoming the exception; and it is only by the irregularity which still pertains to it, aided by the few really antique tenements that remain unaltered, that it now attracts the notice of the curious visitor as the genuine remains of the ancient High Street of the burgh. (*Memorials of Edinburgh in the Olden Time,* Daniel Wilson, 1848)

The Kirkgate was a bustling community of shops and houses – the colourful, pulsating heart of Leith. It was known as the 'Channel' from its length and narrowness – 367 yards

(335 metres) long and 17 yards (15 metres) wide. It was one of the oldest streets of the town, until the 1960s, when progress made its mark and replaced the entire area with modern housing developments, a new shopping centre and a community centre. All that remains of the historic location is Trinity House and South Leith Parish Church.

Trinity House

Trinity House was built on the Kirkgate between 1816 and 1818 as the headquarters of the Fraternity of Masters and Mariners, a charitable foundation for seamen. The current building incorporated the basement and vaults of the former Trinity House and Mariners' Hospital of 1555. The fraternity's original purpose was benevolent, but later it provided pilots for the navigation of the Forth, and was responsible for installing the first guide light on May Island.

Trinity House and the Kirkgate.

Trinity House.

South Leith Parish Church and Leith Tolbooth

South Leith Parish Church in the Kirkgate has its origins in a fifteenth-century chapel dedicated to St Mary. In 1645, the church provided relief to the victims of the plague in Leith when over 2,700 people fell victim to the disease. The colours of the 7th Company of the Scots Guards are kept at the church in memory of the Gretna Rail Disaster. The graveyard is the burial place of John Pew, the inspiration for Blind Pew in the novel *Treasure Island*; Adam Whyte, Leith's first provost; and Hugo Arnot, the Leith historian. The present building is the result of a substantial reconstruction in 1848.

A plaque with the arms of Mary, Queen of Scots, which is now built into porch of South Leith Parish Church, is all that survives of Leith's Tolbooth. It was originally displayed near the parapet above the central pend of the old Tolbooth. The Royal Arms of Mary of Guise (sometimes Lorraine), queen of James V, from her house in Water Street are also on display in the porch of the church.

Tolbooth Wynd was one of the oldest streets in Leith and takes its name from the Leith Tolbooth. The Tolbooth was built in 1564 on the south side of Tolbooth Wynd. Its construction was opposed by Edinburgh Council and it required a royal decree by Queen Mary to enable it to proceed. The Tolbooth served the town as council chamber, tax office, courtroom and jail. The central pend led to the flesh market at the rear, and the prison was above the archway. The building was demolished in 1825, despite protests from Sir Walter Scott.

Tolbooth Wynd, like the Kirkgate, was noted for its bustling character and wide range of shops. The historic stone tenements of Tolbooth Wynd disappeared with the Kirkgate in the comprehensive redevelopment of the 1960s.

South Leith Parish Church.

Above left: Tolbooth Wynd, 1882.

Above right: Leith Tolbooth, 1820.

Right: The royal arms of Mary, Queen of Scots from the Tolbooth, in South Leith Parish Church.

Royal arms of Mary of Guise-Lorraine in South Leith Parish Church.

Cant's Ordinary

Cant's Ordinary, with its arcaded frontage, was a tavern on the old Kirkgate. It was visited by Mary, Queen of Scots, Oliver Cromwell, Charles II and many other notable people, until it was demolished in 1888. The name, Cant's Ordinary, derives from the name of the landlord of the establishment, and the communal method of dining in the tavern. The building that replaced Cant's Ordinary incorporated a commemorative carved stone plaque, which was moved to its current location following the 1960s redevelopment of the Kirkgate.

Cant's Ordinary.

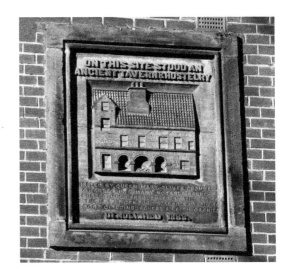

Cant's Ordinary plaque.

Balmerino House

Balmerino House was a large and elegant mansion that stood at the corner of the Kirkgate and Coatfield Lane. The house was built for the Earl of Carrick in 1631 and passed into the ownership of Lord Balmerino in 1643. In July 1650, Charles II spent a night in the house during the defence of the city against Cromwell.

Balmerino House.

5. The People's History of Leith Mural

The people's history of Leith Mural.

The huge mural on the gable of the building on North Junction Street was painted in 1986 by Tim Chalk, Paul Grime and David Wilkinson. It is an evocative celebration of Leith's maritime, social and industrial heritage, and aims to capture the spirit of Leith.

The gap site, which is now an open-air seating area and children's' play area, in front of the Leith mural was the site of a tenement, the upper floors of which held the Corner Rooms. The Corner Rooms hosted all sorts of activities, from Monday night whist drives to dance classes and pipe band practice.

The subjects depicted on the mural were based on the memories of a group of local people.

The Gaiety Theatre

The site of Leith's Gaiety Theatre (the Gaff) on the Kirkgate was originally occupied by a United Presbyterian church. In October 1886, the church moved out and it was purchased by a 'few gentlemen in Leith' who operated the Kirkgate Music Hall from the building. On 2 March 1888, an audience of mainly children had just left the hall, after an exhibition of marionettes, when the building went on fire. The fire spread rapidly, fuelled by the wooden seats in the building, and the conflagration threatened other properties in the densely populated Kirkgate. Panic prevailed in neighbouring premises and residents hurriedly removed portable items of furniture. However, the fire brigade, thanks to a plentiful supply of water and help from soldiers from Leith Fort, were able to prevent the fire spreading and averted the danger of a greater disaster. The hall was totally destroyed and it was fortunate that no lives were lost.

Right: The Gaiety Theatre on the Leith Mural.

Below: The Gaiety Theatre.

On 30 December 1889, H. E. Moss opened the new Princess's Theatre on the site. The new theatre was described as 'handsome and commodious' with a pit and gallery that had accommodation for 1,000 – although the fire escapes were through adjoining ground floor flats. The 'highly realistic drama', *False Lights,* was chosen for the opening performance and it was noted that it 'formed an excellent entertainment'. It was predicted that the theatre would 'undoubtedly become an attractive resort for pleasure seekers'. When Moss's lease on the theatre expired in 1899, he moved on to concentrate on building up his nationwide chain of Empire Theatres.

After alteration and renovation, the theatre reopened on 30 October 1899, as the New Gaiety, in the presence of a large audience. The stage had been enlarged and 'the arrangements for the comfort of the public greatly improved'. A specially commissioned drop scene depicting the unveiling of the statue of Burns in Leith the year before was met with 'hearty applause'. The opening night performance was a 'very intelligent interpretation of the drama called *At the Foot of the Altar,* which laid bare the official corruption and maladministration of justice in Russia.'

The theatre closed in April 1903 and was taken over by the Grand Theatre and Opera House, Glasgow (Ltd). Following a major reconstruction, it opened again on 1 December 1903 with 'the famous American drama *The Fatal Wedding'.* It was billed at the time as the 'handsomest theatre in the district, having been entirely rebuilt'. The accommodation was doubled to around 2,000, the stage was enlarged and a new decorative scheme introduced. 'A Grand Fashionable Night' was held at the theatre on 3 December 1903 with Provost Mackie and the magistrates and councillors of the burgh of Leith in attendance. The occasional talent shows at the Gaiety attracted big crowds of Leithers, to support their neighbours who were displaying their talents on stage.

The theatre was used as a cinema from 1913 and on 3 July 1944, it was reopened as a variety theatre, Will Fyffe performing the opening ceremony. The summer show for the opening year was headed by Tommy Hope, and the Gaiety went on to host some of the major stars of the time. The Gaiety finally closed its doors to the public in September 1956. One of the major attractions in the February of the closing year was Mrs Marie Ashton's, a Manchester housewife's, attempt at the world marathon record for playing the piano. Mrs Ashton set a new world record and collapsed after playing the piano for 132 hours. The building was demolished, along with other parts of the Kirkgate, in the 1960s.

The Docks and Shipbuilding

The original harbour at Leith was a quay at the mouth of the Water of Leith. This was upgraded by the East and West Old Docks in the early nineteenth century. The work was expensive and Edinburgh agreed to the town's independence in 1833 to avoid paying for them. The Victoria Dock followed in 1847–51, the Prince of Wales Graving Dock was added in 1858 and the Albert Dock, which was the first in Scotland with hydraulic cranes, was completed in 1869. The Edinburgh Dock was built for coal delivery in 1877–81, and the final wet dock, the Imperial Dock, was completed 1898. A second large graving dock, the Alexandra, was added beside the Prince of Wales Dock in 1896. The Forth Ports Authority was established in 1968 to control the ports on the Forth, with their headquarters at Leith.

Shipbuilding on the Leith Mural.

On 26 June 1913, 3,000 Leith dock workers went on strike after the Dock Labour Employers refused to concede to their claim for an extra penny on their standard hourly rate of 7*d*. It was an acrimonious and often violent period in Leith's history. There were running battles in the street between strikers and police. It was particularly noted that the women of Leith played a leading part in the disturbances, 'encouraging the men with shouts of approval and joining in the attacks on the police'. Hundreds of troops were held in readiness to quell any rioting, artillery was brought in to Leith Fort and six gunboats were stationed in the docks. The strike ended after a meeting at the Gaiety Theatre on 14 August 1913. The Dock Labour Employers had not given way and the dockers, after months of hardship, voted to return to work without any increase in wages.

Among the industries of Leith, ship-building takes a high place. (*Ordnance Gazetteer of Scotland*, Francis H. Groome, 1885)

During the first half of the nineteenth century, Leith gave promise of being one of the great shipbuilding centres of the country, but the Clyde seems to have drawn the trade away from the Port. One of the oldest shipbuilding firms in Leith was Sime and Rankin's, which built several warships. Their yard, now built on, was opposite the Custom House, but their dry dock, dating from 1720, and the oldest in Leith still remains, between the Shore and Sandport Street, and now forms the repairing dock of Marr and Company. At the Old Dock gates is the yard of Menzies, a firm which has been established for over a century, and which has sent out many fine ships in its day. In 1837, Menzies built the *Sirius*, the first steamship to cross the Atlantic, which she did in eighteen days. The greater part of the new tonnage launched at Leith is usually from the yard of Ramage and Ferguson. Other shipbuilding firms are Hawthorns, Cran and Somerville, Robb, and Morton. Since the war a principal feature of the work of all the firms has been the altering and equipping of vessels surrendered by the Germans. In 1919, for instance, Cran and Somerville alone dealt with over thirty surrendered merchant ships. (*The Story of Leith*, John Russell, 1922)

Shipbuilding at Leith has a long history: the first ship built in Leith was the *Margaret,* which was commissioned by James IV and launched in 1517. The Leith Mural depicts workers at Henry Robb Ltd. Robb's was established in Leith in 1918 and, at the time, was mainly involved in ship repairs. The company expanded over the years and moved into shipbuilding. Their Victoria Yard was situated at the West Pier in Leith Docks. The business was always limited in scale due to the shallow waters of the Forth, and Robb's was notable for building small to medium-sized vessels. During the Second World War, the company built over forty warships.

Robb's provided long-term jobs and apprenticeships in every trade relating to shipbuilding. The workforce numbered in excess of 500 in the 1950s, adapting from its war work to produce cargo ships and utility vessels. Life in Leith's shipyards was demanding. A basic wages of 22s per week was standard for a qualified machine shop worker. Sick pay was non-existent, with workers having to rely on their workmates to

Street games on the Leith Mural.

have a whip-round if they were off work. Christmas Day was a normal working day. In 1955, the company moved from private to public hands. The Robb Caledon yard (the name changed in 1977) closed in 1984 and the land it once occupied was redeveloped as the Ocean Terminal Shopping Centre, home to the Royal Yacht *Britannia*.

Children's Games

Children's street games are represented on the mural by a girl with a gird and cleek (hoop and stick); the idea was to push the gird along using the cleek. The games reflect a more innocent time when children were able to play in the street without the obstacles of traffic and parked cars or mobile phones for parents to check up on them. There were even play streets that vehicles were banned from between 4 p.m. and sunset. Many of the skipping and ball games were accompanied by songs and rhymes, which were part of a long oral tradition. The rhymes could vary from street to street and change from day to day. Most of the games have been lost in more recent years and they represent a vanished time in children's history.

The National Hunger March, 1932

The Edinburgh Marchers Council have made final arrangements for their contingent taking the road to London in the National Hunger Strike against the Means Test. This afternoon, the marchers fall in at the Mound. The procession, headed by the National Unemployed Workers' Movement Band will proceed via Princes Street and Leith Street to the foot of the Walk, where a halt will be called; thence by Duke Street, Easter Road and Abbeyhill to the Canongate; and by High Street and North Bridge to the Mound and on to Haymarket Station. The magistrates have granted permission to take up a collection on the route. In the evening a farewell social for the marchers has been arranged by the women's section of the National Unemployed Workers' Movement to be held in Kinnaird's Hall, Kirkgate, Leith. Tomorrow morning at 10 o' clock the Edinburgh district contingent will parade at the Mound for the send-off. At 10.45 the marchers and supporters will set out in procession for Corstorphine, where a bus is chartered to take the men to Glasgow to join the main contingent from all parts of Scotland. They will be accommodated there for the night, and the whole of the unemployed Scottish marchers will set out for London on Monday morning. (*Edinburgh Evening News*, 24 September 1932)

The National Hunger March of 1932, which is depicted on the mural, was one of a number of similar protests in the 1920s and 1930s against the mass unemployment caused by the Great Depression. Marchers from some of the most badly affected areas of the country converged on London on 27 October 1932 and were met by thousands of supporters. The intention was to present a petition to Parliament objecting to means tested benefits, after a rally in Hyde Park. However, the government, fearing public disorder, mobilised a huge police force and the protest ended in a violent riot.

The National Hunger March on the Leith Mural.

The National Hunger March, 1932.

Moving On

The 1960s brought the final days of what older Leithers would describe as the heart of Leith. The brimming tenements, shops and small workshops along the ancient thoroughfares of Leith were destined for redevelopment. The Kirkgate, St Andrew Street, Tolbooth Wynd, Bridge Street and many more would disappear. The 'modernisation' of Leith in the 1960s followed the 1930s depression, the interruption of the war, and the austerity of the 1950s. When progress came in the 1960s, the face of Leith and the lives of Leithers changed forever.

Moving on.

Leith welcomes new Leithers.

After decades of industrial decline, slum clearance and depopulation in the post-war era, Leith gradually began to enjoy an upturn in its fortunes in the late 1980s. The emphasis moved to urban renewal, community needs and the conservation of Leith's historic buildings. Today, Leith is a thriving port and cruise line destination with many excellent hotels, restaurants and bars. It is also the base of the Royal Yacht *Britannia* and the home of Scotland's Civil Service at Victoria Quay.

Gretna Disaster

'The whole town was stricken with grief, and sore did she mourn her fallen sons.' The incident that most affected Leith during the First World War was the terrible fate of the 7th Royal Scots (Leith's Own) while on its way to join the fighting. The Gretna Rail Disaster occurred at 6.50 a.m. on 22 May 1915 at Quintinshill near Gretna, due to an error by a signalman. The troop train collided with a stationary local train and the north-bound

Left: Gretna Disaster funeral procession on the Leith Mural.

Below: Gretna Disaster funeral procession passing Pilrig Church.

Gretna War Memorial, Rosebank Cemetery.

Euston to Glasgow train ploughed into the wreckage causing further devastation. There were 226 fatalities, the greatest loss of life ever for a rail crash in Britain. The dead included 214 soldiers from the Leith Battalion of the Royal Scots, on their way to Gallipoli. 107 of the dead were brought to the Drill Hall in Dalmeny Street (now Out of the Blue), which was used as a temporary mortuary. Pilrig Street was lined with crowds of people for the funeral procession to Rosebank Cemetery, which took three hours to pass. An annual remembrance service is held at the memorial in the cemetery.

The Leith Pageant

The Leith Hospital Pageant is represented on the mural by Boy Scout and Boys' Brigade bands, and the Leith Bakers in ceremonial dress.

Leith Hospital, which opened in 1851, was dependent for funding on donations and legacies until it was taken over by the NHS in 1948. The pageant was first established in 1907 to raise funds for the ever-expanding Leith Hospital. It was an immensely popular annual event that raised thousands of pounds to support the hospital, 'a deserving institution which won the high regard of the community'. The 'notable efficiency' of the hospital and its ability to meet the increasing demands on its resources was recognised as being due to its 'munificent benefactors and the generosity of the public'. In 1927, it was noted that a 'splendid new wing for the treatment of children had been added, which was of inestimable advantage'.

The Leith Pageant was the big carnival day in Leith. It was supported by all sections of the community and huge crowds lined the route of the procession, which could take three quarters of an hour to pass, as it proceeded from Leith Links through the main streets of the town with hundreds of collectors in fancy costumes 'reaping a ripe harvest' of donations, which were 'heartily given'.

Leith Pageant on the Leith Mural.

Leith bakers in traditional dress in the Leith Pageant.

There was always a variety of 'elaborate exhibits and fine artistic displays in the decoration of the vehicles' that were part of the pageant, with shipbuilding always being well represented. In 1920, the shipbuilders Ramage and Ferguson had eight lorries in the pageant, which included displays of a four-mast sailing ship; a model slipway, with a ship being launched; and a tableaux of riveters at work. In the same year, one of the most popular exhibits was a putting competition on a miniature golf green on the back of a lorry. As many as thirty bands took part and concert parties visited all parts of the town.

Leith Hospital was closed in 1987. However, the spirit of the pageant is maintained by the annual Leith Gala and Festival.

6. Around the Shore

The Shore.

The Shore stretches south from the foot of Tolbooth Wynd along the right bank of the Water of Leith, and presents a single line of houses, some of which bear the marks of a considerable age. It is by far the most picturesque of the streets of Leith, and indeed, but for the familiar names upon the shops and warehouses, might well be mistaken for the quay-side street of some old French town. (*Ordnance Gazetteer of Scotland*, Francis H. Groome, 1885)

The King's Wark
The King's Wark has characteristic Dutch gables and scrolled skewputts in typical early eighteenth-century fashion. It stands on older foundations, which were part of a much larger complex of buildings begun by James I in 1434 to serve as a royal residence with a storehouse, armoury, chapel and tennis court. The reputation of the pub, which occupies the building, was once notorious, and it was known locally as 'The Jungle'. It is now a much more salubrious establishment.

The King's Wark.

Lamb's House.

Andro Lamb's House

Andro Lamb's House in Water's Close is one of the largest and most architecturally impressive seventeenth-century merchant's houses in Scotland. The house takes its name from Andrew Lamb, the first recorded owner and a wealthy Leith merchant. Mary, Queen of Scots 'remainit in Andro Lamb's House be the space of ane hour' when she arrived in Leith on 19 August 1561. In the early twentieth century, the building was subdivided into a number of flats and by the 1930s was in a derelict condition. In 1938, the Marquess of Bute stepped in to buy the building for £200. It was restored by the architect Robert Hurd and in 1958 the building was gifted to the National Trust for Scotland. It was then leased to the Edinburgh and Leith Old People's Welfare Council and used as a day centre for the elderly. It has now been expertly restored as a family home.

The Signal Tower.

The Signal Tower

The signal tower is an important Leith landmark at the corner of the Shore and Tower Street. It dates from the seventeenth century and was built originally as a windmill to process linseed. In 1805, the sails were removed and battlements added. It was used as a signal tower from which flags were displayed to let ships entering the harbour know the depth of water at the harbour bar.

The Sailors' Home

The Sailors' Home at Leith was opened on 29 January 1885 by Lord Roseberry. For many years, sailors visiting Leith had found accommodation at premises on Dock Place. However, these closed in 1881, when the building was taken over by the Mercantile Marine Board and the Government Navigation School. Leith then ceased to have dedicated accommodation for visiting sailors. In June 1882, a subscription was opened with the aim of providing appropriate premises and, in September 1883, the foundation stone of the new building, designed by Charles Johnston in a Scottish Baronial style, was laid. The Sailors' Home provided a dry warm bed for sailors visiting Leith from around the globe. The accommodation included a restaurant, a 'coffee-palace' a recreation hall, storage for the sailors' equipment, a wash house and a laundry on the ground floor. There was an officers' mess, a library, smoking room, reading room and dining room, which could accommodate a hundred, on the first floor. The upper floors included a shop that provided 'all that was needed for Jack ashore' and sleeping compartments for fifty-six sailors and nine officers. Rooms in the attic were kept vacant for use in the event of overcrowding or shipwrecks. The massive square 23-metres- (75-feet-) high tower with a large clock dial was the main feature of the frontage. At the top of the tower there was a

The Sailors' Home.

The Sailors' Home
inscribed panels.

little room with a stove, powerful telescope and all the necessary apparatus for signalling. The building was converted into the Malmaison Hotel in 1994.

Inscribed stone panels on the building commemorate the laying of the foundation stone on 20 September 1883 and the opening of the building by Lord Roseberry on 29 January 1885. The arms of Leith and Edinburgh are also depicted. The head of an angel above the main entrance door is framed by ghost writing that reads Sailors' Home.

The Merchant Navy Memorial

The Merchant Navy Memorial is a 5.5-metres- (18-feet-) high sandstone column at the Shore. It was designed by artist Jill Watson and made at Powderhall Bronze. Jill Watson interviewed a ninety-year-old merchant seaman and other more recent merchantmen as research for the memorial. Leith was selected as the site for the memorial, as it was Scotland's main port for more than 300 years. It was unveiled on 16 November 2010 by Her Royal Highness Princess Anne, patron of the Merchant Navy Memorial Trust Scotland.

The memorial is topped by the Merchant Navy crest (a ship's prow and sails). The column features evocative bronze figures depicting seafaring scenes, which tell the story of Scotland's relationship with the sea and celebrate the many aspects of life in the Merchant Navy in both war and peacetime, including the contribution of Leith Nautical College to the training of merchantmen. Leith Nautical College was originally founded as Leith Navigation School in 1855 at the Mariner's Church in Commercial Street. In 1903, the school moved to purpose-built premises in Commercial Street and changed its name to Leith Nautical College. In 1977, it moved to new premises on Milton Road.

The inscription reads: 'What stands before you commemorates the sacrifice by over 6,500 British Merchant Navy personnel from Scotland in the two World Wars, all other losses in previous and subsequent theatres of conflict and in peacetime duties along the trading routes of the World.'

The Merchant Navy Memorial.

Above: Merchant Navy Memorial detail, showing mooring.

Left: Leith Nautical College.

Bust of John Hunter

John Hunter (1737–1821) was born in Leith and was Governor of New South Wales between 1795 and 1800. The inscription on the bronze plaque attached to the bust reads:

> Governor John Hunter Governor of New South Wales 1795–1800. Born Leith 29th August 1737. Died London 13th March 1821. John Hunter, son of a Leith ship master, was second in command aboard H.M.S. Sirius to Governor Arthur Phillip who founded the colony in January 1788. He returned to be the colony's second Governor and conducted its Government with sense, duty, and humanity. This bust was donated to the Scots Australian Council in Edinburgh by its sculptor, Victor Cusack, and the Scottish Australian Heritage Council in Sydney and was unveiled on 28th August 1994, by the Rt. Hon. Norman Irons, the Lord Provost of the City of Edinburgh, and His Excellency, the Hon. Neal Blewett, High Commissioner for Australia.

Bust of John Hunter.

The Harpoon Gun.

The Harpoon Gun

The harpoon gun on the Shore is a link to Leith's long association with the whaling industry, which was a mainstay of Leith for centuries. Originally focussing on local waters, by the nineteenth century the whaling ships were travelling to the Antarctic. The Christian Salvesen Company's whaling fleet was the largest in the world. Salvesen's headquarters were in Leith and whaling was an important means of employment for Leithers, until Salvesen withdrew from the industry in 1963. Salvesen's whaling stations in the South Atlantic led to the main settlement of South Georgia in the Falklands being named Leith. Although whaling is now a contentious trade, for many years, it was an important part of the Scottish economy, providing raw materials for numerous industries.

Sandy Irvine Robertson Statue

Sandy Irvine Robertson was a wine merchant and founder of the Scottish Business Achievements Awards Trust. He is depicted relaxing on a bench in a life-size bronze sculpture, which was installed in 1999. A plaque on the bench reads: 'Sandy Robertson Irvine OBE. 11th August 1942 – 20th June 1999. Commissioned by his friends. Sculpted by Lucy Poett.'

Sandy Irvine Robertson statue.

DID YOU KNOW?
The octagonal light tower in the background was originally the Burntisland Harbour East Breakwater Light. It dates from 1876 and was moved to the Shore in the 1990s to reflect Leith's maritime heritage.

St Ninian's Chapel and the Bridges

In 1493, Robert Ballantyne, Abbot of Holyrood, built the chapel of St Ninian's, which afterwards became North Leith parish church, and erected a bridge of three stone arches to connect North Leith with South Leith. This was the first bridge thrown across the Water of Leith, and its stability and endurance have been fully proved by the length of time it has been available as a means of crossing the river. (*Ordnance Gazetteer of Scotland*, Francis H. Groome, 1885)

St Ninian's.

Ballantyne's
Bridge.

The Victoria
Swing Bridge.

The former chapel dedicated to St Ninian on the bank of the Water of Leith is the oldest building in Leith. The building fell into ruin after the Reformation, was restored in 1595 and became the church of the new parish of North Leith in 1606. It was rebuilt and extended in the late seventeenth century, when the distinctive steeple was added. In 1816, the congregation moved to a new church in Madeira Street. In 1825, St Ninian's was converted for commercial purposes, as a granary and a mill. It was restored as offices by the Cockburn Association in 1997.

Robert Ballantyne was also responsible for the fifteenth-century stone Brig o' Leith. The tolls collected on the bridge were used for religious and charitable purposes. The Upper Drawbridge (Tolbooth Wynd Bridge), which allowed ships to berth further upstream, replaced the Brig o' Leith in 1787. Its central opening span was fixed in the mid-twentieth century.

DID YOU KNOW?
The Victoria Swing Bridge was opened in 1874 to link the Victoria Dock with the Albert and Edinburgh Docks. It weighs 620 tons, its wrought-iron girders are 65 metres (212 feet) long and the roadway width is 7 meters (24 feet). It was the largest swing bridge in the United Kingdom until the opening of Kincardine Bridge in 1937. The bridge was hydraulically operated to allow ships to pass up the Water of Leith. The bridge no longer swings and the road and the rail tracks have been removed. A new fixed road bridge, immediately downstream of the old bridge, carries motor traffic through to the Ocean Terminal shopping centre.

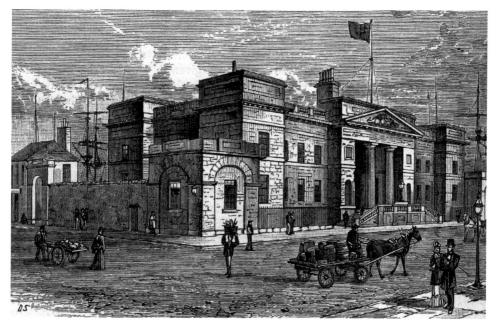

The Leith Custom House.

The Custom House

The Custom House was designed by Robert Reid and opened for the business of collecting duty on goods imported through Leith in 1812. Its Greek Doric Revival style is typical of the way Leith buildings of the period tended to reflect, on a smaller scale, those of Edinburgh's neoclassical New Town. It is located on the site of the old ballast quay and was a replacement for the old Custom House in Tolbooth Wynd. The pediment above the entrance displays the royal coat of arms of George III. From 1980, the building was used as a store by the National Museum of Scotland. It was purchased by Edinburgh Council in 2014 and it is hoped that the future use of the building will include a Leith museum.

The Black Swan

The Black Swan of our day is merely an up-to-date public-house. It lacks all the quaint picturesqueness of its ancient predecessor that used to speak to us so eloquently of its old-world past. The Black Swan of days of yore was the great trysting-place of North Leith. Close by stood the village well where gossiping dames and pretty serving-maids would foregather to fill the household stoups, and exchange pleasantries with the jolly sailor lad who came with water-barrel for the supply that was to serve the ship's crew on the outward voyage. How many a yarn of fights at sea with the French privateers of the old war days, and of the perils of the Greenland whale-fishing, must have been spun within and around the old Black Swan. (*The Story of Leith*, John Russell, 1922)

The original Black Swan was the village inn of North Leith, frequented by old salts spinning tales of the high seas. It was rebuilt in 1892 and continued trading as the Black Swan. Over time the tales changed to those of the perils of whale hunting in the icy seas of South Georgia. In recent years, the Black Swan forfeited its name, which it held for generations, and is now the Roseleaf Café.

The Black Swan.

7. Royal Landings at the Shore

Leith was the port at which royalty generally landed when passing to and from the Continent and elsewhere. At Leith James I and his queen, Jane, daughter of the Earl of Somerset, landed on 20 March 1423; from it James II was borne by sea to Stirling, after his abduction from Edinburgh Castle in 1438; there Mary of Gueldres, queen of James II, landed on 1 April 1449; and Margaret of Denmark, queen of James III, in 1469. Sixty-eight years later Magdalene of France, consort of James V, ' the queen of twenty summer days', landed upon the same pier that was burned by Hertford in 1544. The chronicler records that as soon as her foot touched the ground, the Queen knelt, kissed the ground, and prayed God to bless her adopted people. In 1548 Mary, Queen of Scots, sailed from Leith for France; and there, too, after thirteen years spent at the French court, she landed again in 1561. (*Ordnance Gazetteer of Scotland*, Francis H. Groome, 1885)

Until the railway was widely available, most important visitors to Edinburgh arrived by ship at Leith.

Mary, Queen of Scots

This plaque commemorates the landing in Leith of Marie Stuart, Queen of Scots upon her return from France on 19th August 1561. Placed here by the Marie Stuart Society in the year of the Golden Jubilee of Her Majesty Queen Elizabeth 2002. (Plaque at the Shore)

It was a gloomy misty day that seemed to be grieving in sympathy with her on her separation from her beloved France. She had not been expected till the last days of the month, when the nobles and gentry had been summoned with their honourable companies to welcome her Majesty. No preparation had therefore been made to receive her, but the cannon of her two galleys soon brought out the people in crowds to greet her. She *dynit in Andro Lambis house*, in Leith, before she proceeded to Holyrood Palace. (*The Story of Leith*, John Russell, 1922)

> *After a youth by woes o'ercast,*
> *After a thousand sorrows past,*
> *The lovely Mary once again*
> *Sets foot upon her native plain;*
> *Kneel'd on the pier with modest grace,*
> *And turned to heaven her beauteous face.*

Plaque commemorating Mary, Queen of Scots landing at Leith.

Mary, Queen of Scots landing at Leith.

When the eighteen-year-old Mary, Queen of Scots landed at Leith on the morning of 20 August 1561, it was the first time she had set foot in Scotland since she moved to France at the age of five, the country having been run by regents during her absence. The queen returned to Scotland as a widow following the death of her husband, Francis II of France, in December 1560. She was attended by her four Maries – Fleming, Beaton, Livingstone and Seaton. Despite the religious conflict in the country, she was met with 'the cheers of the people and the boom of the cannon' from a large welcoming crowd in Leith and rode to Holyrood 'amid the acclamations of the serried thousands assembled to do her honour'.

The King's Landing

A great deal of discussion has taken place as to the exact spot on which his Majesty is first to set his foot. The convenience of being able to land at any time whatever, induced those who take the lead to prefer the Chain Pier at Newhaven; and an admirable new line of road from there to Edinburgh has actually been formed. On the other hand, the Magistrates and inhabitants of Leith were naturally very desirous that the King should land at their pier. Leith is the ancient seaport of the Scottish metropolis, and there, in former times, the Scottish Monarchs were uniformly accustomed to land. (*Morning Post*, 10 August 1822)

From an early hour in the morning, Leith presented an extraordinary scene of animation and bustle; and the preparations for his Majesty's reception, which were in the most splendid scale, were fully completed by eleven o' clock. In Constitution Street were ranged the trades of Leith, bearing their respective banners. At the place appointed for the landing, an elegant float was moored. The ascent from this to the quay was by a broad flight of steps leading to a spacious platform covered with grey cloth, with crimson carpeting. A little before 12 o' clock a gun from the royal yacht announced that his Majesty had entered his launch. All the ships in the Roads and the Leith batteries immediately fired salutes, and the air resounded with acclamation from all quarters. The launch entered the harbour at a quarter past 12. His Majesty, in the full dress of a British Admiral, was seated at the stern. As his Majesty entered the harbour the acclamations were redoubled, accompanied by waving of hats and by the handkerchiefs of the ladies, who warmly testified their participation in the general feeling. His Majesty appeared deeply to feel the homage of his dutiful subjects, and testified his gratification, by repeatedly taking off his hat, and bowing on all sides. The Harbour and Roads were covered with pleasure barges and boats of all descriptions, filled with well-dressed ladies and gentlemen, which greatly heightened the beauty of the scene. (*The Caledonian Mercury*, 17 August 1822)

The King's Landing is the place at the Shore where George IV first set foot in Scotland on 15 August 1822. It is marked by a commemorative plate, which includes a crown, and is inscribed in Latin: 'GEO IV REX. O FELICEM DIEM' ('King George IV. O happy day'). It was the first time that a reigning monarch had visited Scotland for many years and was considered a momentous event.

The King's Landing plaque.

The Bank of Leith.

Plaque on the Queen Victoria statue depicting the Queen's visit to Leith on 3 September 1842.

> Leith was crowded beyond all description on the day of the landing; every window was filled with faces, ship's riggings swarmed with human figures, and the very roofs of the houses were covered. The cannon of the ships and battery peeled forth their salutes, and the combined cheers of the mighty multitude filled up the pauses. (*Old and New Edinburgh*, James Grant, 1882)

After being greeted by a host of dignitaries at Leith, the king in an open carriage moved up Leith Walk, past cheering crowds, accompanied by pipe bands and clan regiments in a 'splendid procession'.

Sir Walter Scott had a major influence on the pageantry for the king's visit, in what was described as a 'Tartan Extravaganza' – although the somewhat corpulent king's appearance in Highland dress, wearing flesh coloured tights, was savagely lampooned by the caricaturists of the time.

DID YOU KNOW?
For many years, the anniversary of the King's Landing was celebrated by the Leith Royal Landing Club. On the second anniversary, about 200 members of the Club met at Leith's Exchange Tavern where they were entertained by a choir from the Leith Charity School, and numerous toasts and speeches. The object of the club was to 'perpetuate the glorious 15th August, 1822 which brought the most benevolent man, the most accomplished gentleman and the most powerful Monarch that had ever reigned over these realms, amongst us'.

The king's landing at Leith was commemorated on a bank note issued by the Leith Banking Company. The Leith Banking Company was first established in 1792 by eighteen Leith merchants. The bank prospered in the early nineteenth century and had branches in other parts of the country. The main office of the bank was the elegant classical building, which dates from 1806 and is the centrepiece of Bernard Street. Sir Walter Scott is believed to have been an account holder. In 1842, due to debts, it was merged with another bank to become the Edinburgh and Leith Banking Company. This was later taken over by the Clydesdale Bank.

Fifty years later, almost to the same day of King George IV's landing at Leith, in a curious coincidence, Queen Victoria disembarked in the town on 14 August 1872. The visit was arranged to allow the queen to view the site in Charlotte Square for the memorial to Prince Albert and to visit the studio of sculptor John Steell.

The bronze statue of Queen Victoria at the foot of the Walk is one of Leith's best-known landmarks. The statue was conceived and built under the supervision of the Leith Queen Victoria Statue Fund and was designed by John Stevenson Rhind. Lord Roseberry unveiled the statue in front of a large crowd of 20,000 people on 12 October, 1907. Over the decades many Leithers have gathered to exchange news under the watchful gaze of the queen. A panel on the west side of the statue depicts the queen's visit to Leith on 3 September 1842. She landed at Granton, which had better deep-water facilities and only passed through Leith. It was a major blow to the pride of Leith and spurred on the Dock Commissioners to improve the facilities, with the Victoria Dock opening in 1851.

Czar Nicholas Arrives at Leith

The Emperor and Empress of Russia arrived in their yacht, the *Standart*, at Leith at ten o'clock, anchoring near the Channel Fleet, by which they were saluted. They shortly afterwards were welcomed by the Prince of Wales and the Duke of Connaught, who went out in a paddle steamer. Having lunched together, the Russian Ambassador and Lord Roseberry being also of the party, their Majesties and Royal Highnesses were landed at two o' clock amid naval and military salutes and cordial public demonstrations. Addresses were presented to the Czar and Czarina by the Corporations of Leith and Edinburgh. The Czar wore his uniform as colonel of the Scots Greys, who, in compliment to him, were brought from Hounslow to form his escort. The weather was very wet, but notwithstanding this the party drove in open carriages through the docks and street to the railway station. Both the Emperor and Empress seemed much gratified with their popular reception. The Empress and her baby were especially applauded. A very strong military force lined the streets. The Forth Bridge route north was taken. (*The Derry Journal*, 23 September 1896)

Czar Nicholas II and his wife Alexandra landed at the Victoria Road jetty at Leith on Tuesday 1 September 1896 for a private visit to Queen Victoria at Balmoral (Alexandra was the queen's granddaughter). Two Leith tugs were required to bring their 10 tons of luggage ashore. In order to ensure a smooth drive for the royal party to their train at Junction Road station, the grooves of the railway line on the swing bridge were filled-in with wood and the whole route was covered with 50 tons of Musselburgh sand.

Czar Nicholas arrives at Leith.

8. Mutiny at Leith

The scene of the Leith mutiny.

Yesterday, some drafts of the 71st regiment having mutinied, and refused to embark, an order was sent to the Governor of Edinburgh Castle and the Commanding Officer of the South Fencibles, for a party of 200 men to march to Leith, seize the mutineers, and lodge them in the Castle, there to be detained until further orders. A party of that number, was accordingly detached, under the command of a major, three captains and six sublaterns. On their arrival at Leith, they found about fifty mutineers drawn up with charged bayonets, and their backs to the wall, facing the quay. The major not imagining that so small a body would make any resistance, drew up his men so as to prevent any of the mutineers from escaping, and, attended by a sergeant that spoke Earse, went up to them, stated to them the positive orders he had received and expostulated with them on the folly of any resistance on their part. The sergeant too reasoned with them for some time with the same purpose in their own language; but he soon turned to the major, and entreated him to retire, as they would fire. Upon this the major ordered the divison on the right to present, which they did. In the meantime,

Soldier of the 71st Regiment.

a sergeant obseving one of the mutineers attempting to escape, seized him by the collar, and dragged him from the wall, upon which he received two wounds with a sword or bayonet. Another sergeant was wounded by a musket shot from one of the mutineers; and they advancing with charged bayonets, the firing became general on both sides. Captain Mansfield was unfortunately killed by one of the first shots fired by the mutineers. Two rank and file were killed, and several wounded, two of whom, it is supposed, mortally. The number of mutineers killed and wounded is not as yet ascertained; it is supposed that about fifteen are killed, and above twenty wounded. The party returned to the Castle about seven o' clock with 25 prisoners, several of whom were wounded. (*Caledonian Mercury*, 21 April 1779)

On Tuesday 20 April 1779 in front of Leith's Ship Tavern a fateful clash between soldiers, ostensibly on the same side, but divided by cultures, left the Shore at Leith strewn with the bodies of the dead and wounded. The whole tragic event was witnessed by a large crowd of Leithers.

The men of two Highland Regiments, the 42nd and 71st (the Master of Lovat's Regiment), were aggrieved following an order by their officer, Captain Innes, that they were to join a Lowland Company, the 83rd Glasgow Regiment, which would mean that they would lose the right to wear the kilt and possibly be sent abroad, or even worse to England. In the meantime 'the town's people got among the Highlanders and gave them liquor which made them more mutinous.'

Two hundred South Fencible troops from the Castle were sent to suppress the mutiny. However, despite the efforts of Major Sir James Johnston and a Gaelic-speaking sergeant to negotiate with the Highlanders, a skirmish broke out that left a large number of the Highlanders dead or wounded. Captain James Mansfield and two of the Fencible soldiers were also killed. The remains of Captain Mansfield were brought from Leith with the Regiment of Fencibles as an honour guard and interred in Greyfriar's Churchyard, in what was described as a scene 'at once striking and solemn'.

There are thirty wounded men, by yesterday's affray, at present in the Royal Infirmary. The musket balls have been mostly extracted, and many of the men are expected to recover, though most of them are severly wounded. The number of wounded men suddenly received into the Royal Infirmary, rendering a great supply of old linen necessary – any old linen sent by the humane and charitable, will be gratefully received by the mistress of the hospital. (*Caledonian Mercury*, 21 April 1779)

The Highlanders had arrived at Leith with no ammunition and it was suspected that they had been supplied with a small amount of powder and shot by a well-known local porter, Tinkler Tom, and another man, described as 'stout with a timber leg'. Both men were arrested on suspicion of inciting the mutiny and supplying ammunition to the mutineers. They were sent for trial before the Court of Justiciary and it was noted that 'all the evidence shows that they were guilty of accessory to murder.'

At a three-day court martial at Edinburgh Castle starting on 6 May 1779. Three of the mutineers, Charles Williamson, Archibald McIver and Robert Budge, were tried for instigating and inciting mutiny. The three men were noted as speaking only Earse (a sixteenth–nineteenth-century name for Gaelic) and were 'ignorant of the English tongue'. They were also 'accustomed to the Higland habit, so far as to never have worn breeches'. When the Higland dress was prohibited by an Act of Parliament, following the Jacobite Risings, it was found necessary to 'connive at the use of the philibeg (kilt), provided it was made of stuff of one colour, and not of tartan'. These restriction of language and dress meant that they had to join a Highland regiment, as they had no English and 'could not have marched in normal army dress'. It was also noted at the trial that none of the three men had any ammunition, that McIver and Budge had behaved in an inoffensive manner, and that Williamson was too intoxicated to take much part in the incident. Despite this, the three men were unanimously found guilty of mutiny and instigating others to mutiny. The court, 'having duly considered the evil tendency of mutiny and sedition, especially when taken to such enormous lengths as in the present case, did adjudge that the prisoners be shot to death'.

The three men were on their knees in front of their coffins at the castle waiting to be shot when news of a free pardon granted by the king arrived – 'His Majesty having been pleased to signify His Royal Pleasure, that having regard to the former commendable and distinguishing behaviour of the prisoners is most graciously pleased to grant a free pardon in full confidence that they will endeavour, upon every future occasion, by a prompt obedience and orderly demeanor, to atone for the unpremeditaed but atrocious offence.' The prisoners were noted as being 'sensibly affected by His Majesty's goodness'.

9. Leith Races

Leith Races.

For almost 200 years, from 1620 to 1816, the main venue for horse racing in Scotland was the Leith Sands, a long stretch of beach, which linked up with Leith Links and provided an extensive area for the racing.

The Leith Race week was normally at the end of July or the beginning of August, and was the sporting event of the year in Scotland. The races attracted great crowds of people from all over the country, keeping Leith in a 'state of feverish excitation'.

As the race week was organised by the town council, a uniformed city officer marched to the races every morning, 'bearing aloft at the end of a long pole the gaily-ornamented city purse' and accompanied by a contingent of the City Guard with fixed bayonets. Many of the Race goers chose to 'gaun down wi' the purse' so that the city officer 'disappeared amidst the moving myriads, until only the purse at the end of the pole revealed his presence'.

Great care was taken to have the course measured off and in good order for the horses, and proclamations were issued prohibiting digging for bait until the races were over.

Prizes included the City of Edinburgh purse of £50, His Majesty's purse of 100 guineas and the Ladies Subscription of 50 guineas. On the last day of the meeting, there was a purse for the horses beaten in the earlier part of the week.

The racing seems to have been a sideline to other activities. The scene at Leith was described as 'a vast line of tents and booths stretched along the level shore; recruiting sergeants with their drummers beating, sailors ashore for a holiday, mechanics accompanied by their wives or sweethearts, servant girls, and other motley groups, were constantly passing in and out of the drinking places; the whole varied by shows, rowley-powleys, hobby horses, and wheels-of-fortune.' For an entire week, Leith was 'one continued scene of racing, drinking and fighting'.

The final day of the race meeting was the most outrageous and was usually concluded by the 'general demolition of the stalls and booths and a fighting match amongst those that were able to keep their legs, a riotous brawl being maintained by the returning crowds along the entire length of Leith Walk'. It sounds like a good time was had by most.

In 1816, the horse racing was transferred to Musselburgh Links, as the smooth turf provided an improved track and the docks at Leith had expanded. Later attempts were made to re-establish the Leith Races, but there were significant objections from church groups and others due to the 'drunkenness and excesses' associated with the event. From the following report, in 1840, it also appears that they were a major risk to life and limb.

The second annual effort to revive this ancient amusement (horse racing) at the Port took place yesterday. The turn-out of spectators was as great as we ever remember having seen at Musselburgh. The shore was lined with stalls and tents with refreshments of every description. Nor were the ordinary boyish pursuits awanting, such as merry-go-rounds, and rowley-powleys. The Incorporated Carters with their horses gaily bedizened with coloured ribbons, lined the course, while behind them on each side were ranged a variety of coaches, gigs and other vehicles, chiefly filled with ladies, the whole presenting a scene at once lively and interesting. There was, however, a want of order among the people – which rendered it difficult to keep the course clear, and several accidents were the consequence. A boy was ridden over by one of the horses and nearly killed, and more than one of the riders were thrown, from the sharp turns they were obliged to take to avoid similar accidents. (*Scotsman*, 24 June 1840)

DID YOU KNOW?
The cone-shaped structures in the background of the Leith Races image were associated with Leith's once thriving glassmaking industry. The main glassmakers were grouped around Salamander Street and the street takes its name from the legend of the salamander – the fireproof lizard.

10. Golf at Leith Links

Right: Golf at Leith Links.

Below: The Sabbath Breakers – John Henrie and Pat Rogie.

Golfers Land, Canongate.

Edinburgh, April 6. On Saturday laſt there was a ſolemn Match at Golf in the Links of Leith for 20 Guineas, betwixt Mr. ALEXAN. DER ELPHINGSTON, Son to the Lord BALMERINOCH and Captain Porteous of the Town Guard; when Mr. Elphingſton won His Grace the Duke of Hamilton, the Earl of Morton, and a great ma. ny Perſons of Diſtinction were preſent, beſides a very great Mob.

Caledonian Mercury report of 6 April 1724 of the 'solemn match of golf' on Leith Links.

In the second half of the eighteenth century regular streets, including Bernard Street and Constitution Street, were built on the edges of Leith, and Queen Charlotte Street was cut through the medieval layout of the town. Leith became a fashionable seaside resort, which, as early as 1767, included a golf clubhouse built by the Honourable Company of Edinburgh Golfers at the west end of the Links. Duke Street was named after the Duke of Dalkeith in 1812 – the Duke was an enthusiastic golfer and rented a house in the area to be close to the course at Leith.

Cockfighting.

Leith Links was part of a larger area of common land that stretched along the coast including part of Seafield. Links means sandy ground with hillocks and dunes, and the present artificial flatness dates from around 1880, when the Links were remodelled into a formal park. These improvements removed most of the world's oldest golf course, which is mentioned as early as 1457.

In 1593, the town council noted that a number of inhabitants of Edinburgh were heading down to Leith Links 'at the time of the sermons to partake of archery and golf, thereby profaning the Sabbath day'. They were warned to desist or be punished by the magistrates. However, the threat of punishment did not divert John Henrie and Pat Rogie, two early martyrs to the law, from their passion for the game. In 1608, Henrie and Rogie were imprisoned for the 'playing of the gowff on the Leith Links every Sabbath'. P. G. Wodehouse dedicated his book of golf stories *The Clicking of Cuthbert* to the 'immortal memory of John Henrie and Pat Rogie'.

James VI, in 1618, and Charles I, in 1633, eased the restrictions on recreational activities on the Sabbath, noting that 'as the common people only have leave to exercise on a Sunday, as they must apply their labour and win their living on working days, they should not be disturbed from any lawful recreation after the end of divine service.'

DID YOU KNOW?
The first rules of golf, which are the basis of the modern game, were drawn up in 1744 for use on the Links by Leith's Honourable Company of Edinburgh Golfers. The two raised knolls, the Giant's Brae and Lady Fyfe's Brae, at the western end of the Links are believed to be artillery mounds, Somerset's Battery and Pelham's Battery, used during the 1560 siege of Leith. There is a theory that the golf warning 'fore' may have derived on Leith Links from the old Scottish military warning – 'ware-before' – for the firing of artillery.

In 1681, the Duke of York, the future James VII of Scotland/II of England, and John Patersone, a local golf ball maker and skilled golfer, easily beat two English noblemen on the Links in what was possibly the first international golf match. Patersone built Golfer's Land in the Canongate with his share of the winnings. The house was demolished in the 1960s and is now commemorated by a plaque.

A report in the *Caledonian Mercury* of 6 April 1724 of the 'solemn match of golf' on Leith Links between Alexander Elphinstone and John Porteous is considered to be the first ever coverage of a golf match in a newspaper. Alexander Elphinstone was the winner. Some twelve years later, John Porteous who was Captain of the City Guard, got on the wrong side of the Edinburgh mob and was lynched in the Grassmarket. It was also not Alexander Elphinstone's last public appearance on Leith Links. On 23 December 1729, he was involved in a duel on the Links with Lieutenant John Swift of Lord Cadogan's Regiment. The duel was due to the most 'opprobrious and abusive language given Mr Elphinstone by Lieutenant Swift' and they met next morning on Leith Links to decide the affair. The result was fatal for Lieutenant Swift and Elphinstone was badly wounded. He was apprehended by a group of soldiers, but, despite his wounds, was able to escape. The case never came to trial and Elphinstone passed away at his father's house in Coatfield Lane three years after the duel.

Leith Links was also the scene of less savoury activities than golf. Cockfighting was introduced into Edinburgh by William Mauchrie, a teacher of fencing and cockfighting in Edinburgh, in the first years of the eighteenth century. Mauchrie published an *Essay on the Innocent and Royal Recreation and Art of Cocking*, in which he noted that he had 'a special veneration and esteem for those gentlemen, about Edinburgh, who have propagated and established the Royal recreation and innocent pastime of cocking to which they have erected a cock-pit on the Links of Leith.' Admission was 10*d* for a ringside seat, 7*d* for the second row and 4*d* for the back row. An advert in the *Caledonian Mercury* promoted a cockfight in Charles Liddell's cockpit at Leith on the 1 January 1752 – which must have been a particularly unpleasant way to start the New Year.

Edinburgh magistrates banned cockfighting on the streets, 'in consequence of the tumults it excited and the cruel extent to which its practice had been carried'. Despite this ban, cockfighting continued in Edinburgh well into the nineteenth century. Regular cockfights, or mains as they were termed, were held in a cockpit on Leith Sands in 1804. John Kay, the Edinburgh artist, wrote in 1785 that he found it 'surprising that noblemen and gentlemen, in the prosecution of this barbarous sport, demean themselves so far as to associate with the very lowest characters of society'. This 'school of gambling and cruelty' was finally outlawed in the nineteenth century and by 1869 the Society for the Prevention of Cruelty to Animals was able to report that it was now 'the barbarity of a bygone age'. Although in the same year a Leith man was fined for his involvement in a cockfight.

DID YOU KNOW?
In 1645, during the outbreak of the plague, those affected by the disease were banished to huts on Leith Links and they were the last resting place of hundreds of casualties of the disease, which wiped out half of the population of Leith.

11. Leith Citadel

The Citadel Port.

The arch in Dock Street was the main entrance to the seventeenth-century Leith Citadel. In 1650, Cromwell's army occupied Leith after their victory at the Battle of Dunbar. In 1656, a large fort, Leith Citadel, and barracks were built. The Citadel, 'passing fair and sumptuous', was erected on the site of the Chapel of St Nicholas at the foot of Dock Street. It was pentagonal in form with five bastions. The house over the archway, according to tradition, was the meeting place of the officers and men of Cromwell's Ironsides in Leith.

12. The Porters Stone

The tablet of the Association of Porters, over the entrance to the Old Sugar House Close, is extremely interesting, since it shows pictorially how the wine ships that came into Leith were unloaded by a treadmill apparatus, and in what way the casks were carried about from place to place. (*Ordnance Gazetteer of Scotland*, Francis H. Groome, 1885)

Leith has a long history as a centre for the import and maturing of wine. The Vaults on Henderson Street, which are now the home of the Malt Whisky Society, were central to the trade for centuries. A replica, dating from 1990, of Leith's historic Porters Stone is built into the front boundary wall of the Vaults – the original stone is held by the Museum of Edinburgh. The stone is dated 1678 and was located over the entrance to Candlemakers Close (Old Sugarhouse Close) on Tolbooth Wynd. The stone depicts the import of wine to Leith, and shows a two masted carvel, a warehouse, a crane bringing casks ashore powered by a youth on a treadmill and two wine porters carrying a cask slung on a pole. The Leith porters, 'stingmen', transported the wine casks on a pole known as a sting. The porters were one of the many important and powerful trade guilds of Leith's past.

The Porters Stone at Candlemakers Close.

The Porters Stone.

The replica of the Porters Stone.

13. John Sakeouse: Leith's Inuit (Eskimo)

In August 1816, Hans Zakaeus, who was known in Scotland as John Sakeouse, a native of Disko Bay on the west coast of Greenland, landed at Leith aboard the British whaling ship, the *Thomas and Ann.* There are different accounts of how he ended up on the ship. He may have stowed away, although given that he arrived with his kayak, it is perhaps more likely that he was swept out to sea and was picked up by the crew of the ship.

He was a youth of around eighteen and the crew came to be on good terms with Sakeouse. The skipper, Captain Newton, was all for returning him to his home. However, John insisted that he wanted to be taken to Scotland. He was one of the first Eskimos (Inuits) ever to visit Scotland and, on his arrival at Leith, immediately became a source of curiosity.

The curious locals were soon given the opportunity to have a closer look at Sakeouse when he gave a demonstration of his skills with his kayak and harpoon in the Wet Dock at Leith Docks. Dressed in his native costume, he demonstrated feats of agility in the kayak: diving to turn the keel directly upwards, submerging the canoe above him and surfacing again sitting in it. He also beat a six-oared whaleboat in a race and threw his spear at a target with 'unerring accuracy' – he could split a ship's biscuit floating in the water with his harpoon. These exhibitions of 'several feats of dexterity' attracted great attention and resulted in the 'greatest concourse of spectators ever known to have assembled in Leith' with 'not a part of the pier, the windows and roofs of houses, but were crowded; the latter at the imminent risk of many lives'.

John, or Jack as he was affectionately known, soon settled in Leith, lodging with Captain Newton and his family, and was a popular figure in the local community. In the spring of 1817, it was decided that John should be given the chance to return to his home in the Davis Strait and he set sail again on the *Thomas and Ann.* However, his sister, his only relative in Greenland, had died during his time away and he made it clear that he wanted to return to Leith. Back in Leith, John started to learn English and had his portrait painted by Alexander Nasmyth (1758–1840). John also proved skilled at drawing and painting.

In 1818, John embarked on a British Admiralty-organised voyage to search for a Northwest Passage. The expedition was unsuccessful, but John made an invaluable contribution to the expedition as official interpreter and mediator with the natives of Prince Regent's Bay. John also made some watercolour sketches of events on the journey, which were used to illustrate the book describing the expedition, *A Voyage of Discovery to the Arctic Regions in Search of the North-West Passage in His Majesty's Ships Isabella and Alexander, by Captain John Ross (1777–1856), the renowned Arctic explorer.*

On his return, John spent some time in London, but soon tired of the big city and returned to his old friends in Leith. Sadly, he contracted typhoid fever and, despite being treated by some of the most eminent doctors of the time, passed away on 14 February 1819 at the age of twenty-two. A large gathering of John's Leith friends attended his funeral. However, the location of his interment is unknown.

John Sakeouse.

John Sakeouse in his kayak.

14. John Home

John Home plaque, No. 28 Maritime Street.

A small bronze plaque over the entrance door of No. 28 Maritime Street is inscribed: 'The Rev. John Home, author of "Douglas", born here 2nd September 1722'. The plaque was originally displayed on No. 19 Maritime Street (previously known as Quality Street), which was demolished for the Bell's Court development. It also seems that there may be some dispute over the information on the plaque, as various different dates are given for the exact day of Home's birth in September 1722, and there is some claim to Ancrum in Roxburghshire as his birthplace.

Home was a colourful character: soldier, clergyman, dramatist, historian, private secretary to a prime minister and tutor to the Prince of Wales.

Home's father was Leith's town clerk and he was educated at Leith Grammar School. He trained in theology at Edinburgh University, was appointed to the ministry in 1745 and, in the same year, he enlisted as a volunteer in the Hanoverian army. He was captured by the Jacobites at the Battle of Falkirk, but made a dramatic escape from Doune Castle. In 1746, he was appointed as minister of the parish of Athelstaneford in Haddingtonshire (East Lothian), where he is said to have 'cultivated absenteeism' to follow his real passion for literature and poetry, 'having become enamoured to the idea that he was a dramatic genius'.

On 14 December 1756, his blank verse tragedy *Douglas* was premiered at the Canongate Playhouse in Playhouse Close, which was Scotland's first custom-built theatre. The play was met with such unrestrained enthusiasm that a member of the audience is reputed to have called out, 'Whaur's yer Wullie Shakespeare noo'. *Douglas* was produced in London's

John Home
sculpture on the
Scott Monument.

Drury Lane in 1758, which was an overwhelming success and made Home the most popular tragic author of his time. David Hume hailed him as superior to Shakespeare and it was reported that there was 'no equal to Home in the modern, and scarcely a superior in the ancient drama'. Although Samuel Johnson noted that 'he could not fine ten good lines in the whole play' and none of Home's other dramatic works were a great success. The reception for his tragedy *Alfred, in* 1778, was so lukewarm that he abandoned writing for the stage. Time has not been kind to Home's work and an attempt to revive *Douglas* at the Edinburgh Festival in 1950 with Dame Sybil Thorndike in a lead role was met with critical reviews. It was said that 'Home of all Scots men of letters was the most belauded during his lifetime, and the most derided after his death.'

Home's life as a minister-dramatist was impossible at the time, with his passion for the drama resulting in conflict with the church and he resigned from the ministry – his final sermon on 5 June 1757 'drew tears from many of the congregation'. In 1758, he was appointed private secretary to Lord Bute and was tutor to the Prince of Wales, the future George III, who gave his old teacher a substantial pension when he ascended the throne. In 1763, Home was elected MP for Edinburgh.

In 1778, he joined a regiment formed by the Duke of Buccleuch. He retired after a horse-riding accident and in 1802 published his *History of the Rebellion of 1745,* which was noted as being biased against the Jacobites.

Home was famed for the lavish hospitality, which he provided at his house in Edinburgh's Merchiston. David Hume, Adam Smith and Sir Walter Scott were just a few of his eminent friends. He is said to have possessed a magnetic personality and it was noted that 'Home's entry into a company was like opening a window and letting the sun into a dark room.'

Home died at his Edinburgh home in September 1820 and is interred at South Leith Parish Church. He has the distinction of being one of the literary figures depicted in stone on the Scott Monument.

15. The Martello Tower

The Martello Tower.

The Martello Tower at Leith is about to be fitted with cannon, and three guns, 32 pounders, have been sent from Woolwich arsenal, and are now in the docks. The tower was erected during the late war, and cost £10,000. The building was intended to defend the entrance of the harbour of Leith. The form of the tower somewhat resembles a peck, broader at the base than at the top, and somewhat oval in conformation. A tower stood at a place called Mortella, which gave singular trouble to some war ships, and suggested the creation of such structures in this country. A large number of these works are set down on the British coast, but we apprehend they were rather intended for signals in case of danger than defence against an enemy. What kind of resistance might be made by the work to an enemy is of course untested. (*Western Daily Press,* 15 September 1858)

DID YOU KNOW?
Martello towers are defensive structures that were built around the coast during the Napoleonic Wars in the early years of the nineteenth century. They were typically garrisoned by an officer and up to twenty-five men to operate a cannon on the flat roof. The drum shape of the Martello towers was inspired by a round fortress at Mortella Point in Corsica.

Leith's Martello Tower, known locally as the 'Tally Toor', was built on offshore rocks called the Mussel Cape, in 1809, to defend the new docks. With its 2-metres- (6-feet-) thick walls, it was a formidable defence. When the threat of a French invasion passed, the tower was abandoned until the late 1850s, when there were serious concerns that France, under Napoleon III, with the increasing strength of its battle fleet, might attempt to invade.

The tower is now landlocked within the eastern breakwater.

The Martello Tower.

16. The Corn Exchange, Constitution Street

The foundation stone of the new Leith Corn Exchange was laid on the 16th October 1860 by his Grace the Duke of Atholl, the Grand Master Mason of Scotland, amidst all the pomp and display attendant on the gathering of Masonic orders; and the day was observed as a general holiday throughout the town. (*Illustrated Times*, 3 November 1860).

Laying the foundation stone of the Leith Corn Exchange.

The Leith Corn Exchange is now nearly completed. At an additional cost of somewhere about £80, the Constitution Street side of the building has been greatly relieved by a deep belting, tastefully and appropriately carved out into figures and designs illustrative of the conjoined enterprise of agriculture and commerce. (*Caledonian Mercury*, 27 August 1862).

The domed Corn Exchange was at one time the hub for the trading of grain in Scotland. The building dates to 1862 and includes a distinctive frieze on the Baltic Street frontage, which shows cherubs involved in a range of activities associated with the production and marketing of grain. The Corn Exchange was so spacious that it was often used as a drill hall by the entire battallion of Leith Rifle Volunteers in the nineteenth century.

The Corn Exchange.

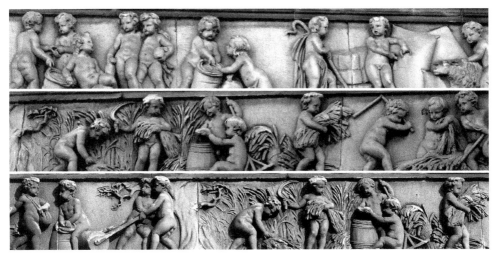

Frieze details on the Corn Exchange.

17. The First Christmas Season Card

WISHING YOU A MERRY CHRISTMAS AND A HAPPY NEW YEAR

The Leith New Year card.

When the first New Year card made its appearance just a century ago, it preceded the first Christmas card by two years. Thomas Sturrock of Leith designed that pioneer Ne'erday greeting, and a Leith printer undertook the publication. That was at the end of 1842. The original Christmas card for which the English artist, Dobson, was responsible, followed in 1844. (*Daily Record*, 26 December 1942)

Leith has some claim to being the home of the Christmas season greeting card. In 1842, Charles Drummond, a bookseller, sold copies of a New Year card from his shop in the Kirkgate. The card featured the 'curly head of a boy, with chubby cheeks, merry twinkling eyes and an expression of hearty laughter'. The illustration had been drawn by local man Thomas Sturrock and engraved by Alexander Aikman. Hogmanay was a more important holiday than Christmas in Scotland at the time, although it was later discovered that there were versions of the card with the message 'Wishing You a Merry Christmas and a Happy New Year' added to the illustration.

18. The Robert Burns Statue and the Gladstone Family

Robert Burns (1759–96), the national bard of Scotland, is depicted in more statues around the world than any other literary figure. Leith's statue of Burns stands on a red sandstone and granite plinth on Bernard Street and portrays Burns with a plaid over his shoulder. It was commissioned by the Leith Burns Club. A 'holiday mood' prevailed as thousands gathered on Bernard Street on 15 October 1898 for the unveiling of the statue by Mr R. C. Munro Ferguson, MP. In 1961, the statue was moved 5.5 metres (18 feet) to the west, to ease the flow of traffic at the junction. In 2004, the statue was again moved a short distance, to take centre stage in a new pedestrian area.

DID YOU KNOW?
The statue is by the eminent Ratho-born sculptor David Watson Stevenson (1842–1904), who, in 1900, had sculpted a bust of four times Liberal Prime Minister William Ewart Gladstone (1809–98). It is, therefore, perhaps no coincidence that the figure of the blacksmith on the plaque illustrating the poem 'Scotch Drink' bears a striking resemblance to Gladstone, who was Leith's Member of Parliament.

The Gladstone family had close connections with Leith and Gladstone Place was named for the family in 1879, the year before WE Gladstone became Prime Minister for the second time. Thomas Gladstones (1732–1809), William's grandfather, was a prosperous Leith corn merchant. Sir John Gladstone (1764–1851), William's father was born on 11 December 1764 in Leith, which is commemorated by a plaque, erected by the Leith Liberal club in 1909, on the corner of King Street and Great Junction Street. Sir John dropped the final 'S' from the family surname.

Sir John made a fortune trading in corn, cotton and sugar out of Liverpool. His sugar plantations in Demerara were worked by slave labour and he was one of the world's largest owners of slaves. This is reflected in the payment of £47,442 14s 6d, which he received as compensation for the loss of his 880 slaves, following the Slavery Abolition Act of 1833 – an amount that represents many millions in today's terms. He was, therefore, easily placed financially to fund philanthropic activities in his birthplace including the construction of the former St Thomas's Church on Sheriff Brae in memory of his wife. In 1976, the building found new life as the Guru Nanak Gurdwara Sikh Temple. Sir John also financed a hospital for incurably sick women in Leith.

Statue of Burns.

Scotch drink plaque on the statue of Burns.

Left: William Ewart Gladstone.

Below: Sir John Gladstone plaque.

SITE OF BIRTHPLACE OF
Sir JOHN GLADSTONE, Bart. 1764
FATHER OF THE
Rt. Hon. WILLIAM EWART GLADSTONE, M.P.
BORN 1809
FOUR TIMES PRIME MINISTER.

THIS TABLET ERECTED BY THE
LEITH LIBERAL CLUB
1909

Right: Sir John
Gladstone.

Below: Former
St Thomas' Church on
Sheriff Brae.

19. The Leith Ragged Industrial School

LEITH INDUSTRIAL SCHOOLS,

57 LOCHEND ROAD, LEITH.

FIREWOOD DEPARTMENT.

THIS Department has always been a special feature in the industrial work of the School, and to meet the ever-increasing demand, extensive Machinery has been erected, which enables all Orders to be promptly executed.

No Wood is used but the BEST NEW RED WOOD that can be obtained in Russia, Norway, or Sweden,—no old or inferior Wood being used,—and *Public Departments, Families, Offices, Banks, Hotels, etc.,* may rely upon being supplied with Wood of the best quality, free from danger of vermin or infection, and at strictly moderate prices, which can be had on application to Superintendent.

Wood supplied either in bundles by the hundred, or unbundled by cwt.

Sent daily (free of Charge) to all parts of Edinburgh, Leith, Trinity, etc. Special terms for large quantities. A Trial solicited.

TURNING DEPARTMENT.

This Department is carefully attended to. All kinds of PLAIN TURNING at very moderate rates. *Special Rates for File and other Handles.* Orders promptly executed. Estimates given. Communications to the SUPERINTENDENT. 57 LOCHEND ROAD. will receive immediate attention.

Leith Industrial School.

The Leith Ragged Industrial School was established in premises on King Street in 1861. The object of the school was the 'boarding of children who, through poverty or neglect were orphans or, through any other cause, were destitute and homeless'. Children were also committed by the courts for detention at the school. In 1869, the school moved to new custom-built premises at Lochend Road. The children were trained in gardening, agriculture, tailoring, shoemaking, wood turning and wood chopping.

By all accounts, it seems to have been a well organised and valuable institution. However, for a spell in the autumn of 1880 there were reports of disturbances, insubordination and even mutiny at the school. In September 1880, a group of 40–50 parents gathered outside the school and broke windows. This incited the boys to rebellion and what was described as a 'serious mutiny'. The boys had the school in uproar, were armed with sticks, and broke more windows. Six of the boys were remanded on a charge of disorderly conduct and were sentenced to twenty days imprisonment by the Leith Police Court. In October 1880, twenty boys absconded from the school by clambering over the surrounding wall, 'evading the notice of the officials in charge in a skilful and successfull escape'. In later years, things seemed to have calmed down, and the school's brass band provided entertainment in local parks and other venues in the Leith area.

The school closed on 31 March 1924 due to dwindling demand. It was noted that during its 'long and most useful existence about 98 per cent of the thousands of children that passed through the school had turned out good and useful members of society'.

DID YOU KNOW?
Ragged schools were dedicated to the education of impoverished children. Thomas Guthrie (1803–73) was one of the leading lights in the ragged school movement. Guthrie was born in Brechin and educated at Edinburgh University. He was minister at Greyfriars Kirk and became moderator of the Free Church assembly in 1862. In 1847, he published 'A Plea for Ragged Schools' and set up a school for 'ragged children'.

A workroom in an Industrial School.

20. The Leith Provident
Co-operative

Inscribed stones on the Leith Provident Building, Great Junction Street.

Before the advent of supermarkets in the 1960s, most shopping was done in local shops – many of which would have been run by one of the retail co-operative societies. In 1950, 10 per cent of all shops in Scotland were owned by retail co-operative societies, and most day-to-day shopping was done in the shops of Edinburgh's two large co-operative societies – St Cuthbert's and Leith Provident.

The Leith Provident Co-operative was established in Leith in 1878, with the first shop opening at No. 147 Great Junction Street. By 1879 the business was doing so well that another shop was rented on Bonnington Road. In 1911, Leith Provident built the large corner tenement building with an imposing domed corner clock tower on Great Junction Street as its flagship store. By 1926, there were twenty-six branches of the Leith Provident, and in 1953 the society had 30,500 members and an annual turnover of £2.5 million.

Leith Provident Building,
Great Junction Street.

In 1975, Leith Provident merged with the St. Cuthbert's Co-operative Association. St Cuthbert's changed name to the Scottish Midland Co-operative Society, or Scotmid for short, in 1981.

Leith Provident inscribed stone on Dalmeny Street.

21. The German Kultur Panel

The German Kultur panel.

In Pitt Street there is presently in course of erection a building which for generations to come is bound to be regarded with peculiar interest, because of a large panel depicting *German Kultur,* which has been placed on the pediment. The panel contains no fewer than eighteen figures, executed in terra cotta from the clay model, and the designer, Mr William Baxter, has been wonderfully successful in portraying with grim reality the savagery and fiendish cruelty of the German soldiery towards the harmless peasants of Belgium. The helpless women and babes are seen being butchered by the merciless Huns, one of whom has his breast adorned with Iron Crosses, no doubt in recognition of previous butcheries in which he has taken part. The postures and facial expressions are striking, and altogether there is a vivid realism about the panel that says much for the artistic skill of Mr Baxter. As a recruiting agency it ought to exert some influence in the burgh, for it ought surely to impress upon the beholder the fact that if this country is to be preserved from such harrowing scenes as that depicted, every man possible should enlist at the present time. It is understood that Mr Baxter has executed copies of the panel for England and Ireland, and he is presently engaged on five war panels, representing land and sea fights. (*Leith Observer,* 3 July 1915)

The scene on the panel, which is inscribed with the sarcastic inscription 'The Valour of German Culture 1914', and the news report from the July 1915 edition of the *Leith Observer* reflect the British attitude towards the German army in the early years of the First World War, following the policy of *Schrecklichkeit* (terror), which was a widely reported aspect of German actions during the invasion of Belgium in 1914. This included the destruction of the medieval city of Louvain and the execution of civilians, as reprisals for local resistance to the invasion. There have been discussions about the extent of the German terror over the years and it was certainly highlighted, at the time, as British anti-German propaganda to encourage enlistment.

The German Kultur panel.

22. The Zeppelin Raid on Leith

Zeppelin L9, which is identical to the Zeppelin that bombed Leith.

The Zeppelin bomber attack on Edinburgh and Leith, on the night of 2 April 1916, brought the First World War to the home front. It caused considerable damage to property and tragic loss of life. Reporting of the attack was subject to censorship during the war years and an item appeared in the *Sunday Post* newspaper in February 1919 under the headline 'Story Now Told for the First Time'.

> It was early in the evening of Sunday April 2 1916, when the alarm reached Edinburgh and Leith that a Zeppelin was heading towards the Forth. Electric lights were lowered, and tramcars were stopped, though with regard to the trams, that was not an unusual occurrence. The interval of waiting, which extended to several hours, was trying but it was curiosity more than fear that exhausted the patience of many people, until at least it was generally considered that the alarm was to be false, and many retired, though before midnight the majority got a rude awakening. It is, however, on record that there were citizens who slept through the raid. (*Sunday Post, February 1919*)

It was a clear night when the Zeppelin was first sighted over the Forth at 11.25 p.m. on the night of 2 April 1916. The long cigar-shaped craft made its way stealthily over the Firth and across the west end of the Edinburgh Dock. The first bomb dropped into the dock, sank two small boats lying beside the quay and damaged two foreign ships. Some damage to the roof of a warehouse in Timberbush and a hole in the wall of the quay in front of the Seamen's Institute were caused by two high-explosive bombs. The first fatality of the raid

Count Zeppelin in civilian dress in the gondola of a German airship.

was Robert Love, aged sixty-six, who was killed by shrapnel at his home on Commercial Street. The other fatality in Leith was a little boy, aged one, who was lying in a crib in a house in Bonnington Road; the bomb landed in the adjacent court and shrapnel hit the sleeping baby inflicting fatal injuries.

The occupants of the manse at St Thomas's Church had narrow escapes – an incendiary bomb struck the roof, and eventually set fire to the staircase. Revd Mr and Mrs Fleming, and their maid, just managed to get downstairs before the staircase burst into flames. Several bombs landed dangerously near the Leith Infirmary, but the building, where a large number of wounded soldiers were being treated, was not damaged. An incendiary bomb, which landed in a tenement in Church Street, went right through a flat occupied by a soldier's wife and her three children, and down into a house where there was a family of seven. Both houses were set on fire, but no one was injured. Three incendiary bombs landed in Sandford Street, one in a tenement, the second on the pavement, and the third in a yard, but none of these caused serious damage. Another incendiary bomb, which fell in the Bonnington district, was found intact, wedged between two railway sleepers. Another bomb fell through the roof of a tannery and landed in a tank of water. The most damage was the result of a bomb that fell on the bonded store of Innes & Grieve.

The Zeppelin continued its course towards Edinburgh, dropping bombs around the Castle, in the Grassmarket, Lauriston Place, Marchmont and on the South Side. The bomb that fell on Marshall Street on the South Side resulted in the greatest numbers of fatalities and injuries.

DID YOU KNOW?

The Zeppelins were developed by Count Von Ferdinand Zeppelin (1838–1917). Zeppelin was a soldier and when he retired from the military in 1890, he turned his attention to aeronautics. In 1990, his first airship was built. After a number of disappointing trials, he developed a design, in 1906, that flew 60 miles in two hours. By the start of the First World War, they were capable of flying long distances and Germany had a fleet of Zeppelins, with which they intended to spread terror in France and Britain. Although there were a number of raids by the Zepps during the First World War, they were never very effective war machines. Their huge size made them vulnerable targets; several were shot down in flames by aircraft and they were obsolete by the end of the conflict.

DID YOU KNOW?

During the debate on Edinburgh Corporation's bill for the extension of the boundary of Edinburgh to include Leith before a House of Lords Select Committee in April 1920, the jealousy between the fire brigades of Edinburgh and Leith was discussed. It was noted that sometimes, when an Edinburgh fire engine was called to a fire close to the boundary, they were told by the Leith Brigade, 'This is not your job; it is ours.' This was even the case at the time of the Zeppelin raid, when bombs were dropped on Leith docks and warehouses were ablaze, the Edinburgh fire engines were not called because they belonged to the Edinburgh Brigade. This was put forward as an argument that Leith, which was surrounded on all sides by Edinburgh and bounded on the other by the sea, should not 'remain an island'.

23. Gibson's Aeroplanes

The successful flights of the Wright Brothers in 1903 encouraged an international aviation enthusiasm. The first recorded powered flight in Scotland was made by Harold Barnwell (1878–1917) on 28 July 1909 in a biplane powered by a car engine. The plane travelled 75 metres (240 feet) at an altitude of around 4 metres (13 feet) over a field

HENRY FARMAN BIPLANE BUILT AT GIBSON'S AEROPLANE WORKS

GIBSON'S AEROPLANES
Aeroplane Designers and Builders

Successful Exhibitors at———
OLYMPIA, LONDON, and
BRUSSELS EXHIBITION

We manufacture Aeroplanes from our own
drawings, or to suit Customers' requirements

Complete Biplanes, all on, from **£450**

GIBSON'S AEROPLANES
109 LEITH WALK, LEITH

WORKS———10 MANDERSTON STREET, LEITH

Gibson's Aeroplanes advert, 1901.

at Causewayhead near Stirling, before it crashed. However, the distinction of the first Scottish flight was very nearly taken by John Gibson (1857–1935), a Leith man who had an adventurous life. His father was a fish curer in Fisherrow and Andrew Gibson, his brother, was a Leith baillie. In his early days, John served on sailing ships and was shipwrecked in an open boat for eighteen days off Cape Horn. He tried his luck for a time at the height of the Australian gold rush before setting up as a fish salesman in Newhaven.

From 1897, John built a substantial business as a bicycle manufacturer and motor engineer in Leith. He took a keen interest in aviation when it was in its infancy and built several planes. It was even possible to pop in to Gibson's shop and buy a plane. A biplane, which he developed at his Leith workshop on Manderston Street, caught fire before a test flight in 1909. Undaunted by this set back, one of Gibson's planes took to the air at Buteland Farm, Balerno in December 1910.

The company was building a new biplane to take part in a challenge race from Glasgow to Edinburgh in 1914, but, with the outbreak of the First World War, Gibson's interest in aviation diminished and the firm turned to other engineering ventures. Gibson died at his house at No. 19 Pilrig Street in August 1935. A propeller from a Gibson plane is held in the collection of the Museum of Flight at East Fortune.

GIBSON'S AEROPLANES
Aeroplane Designers and Builders

Planes, Tails, Ailerons, supplied on receipt of measurements and other details on very short notice.

Best materials only used. Your orders solicited for Scottish-built Planes.

Spare parts or complete machines.

Wood Spars cut any length, straight-grained and free from knots.

Aeroplane Fabric, all grades, at factory prices.

We make Aluminium castings from customers' patterns or drawings. Wood patterns made to order.

We undertake Aeroplane repairs.

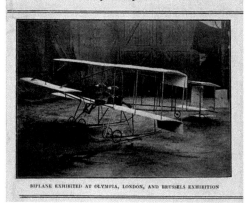

BIPLANE EXHIBITED AT OLYMPIA, LONDON, AND BRUSSELS EXHIBITION

Gibson's Aeroplanes advert, 1901.

24. Leith Airport

Sir Alan Cobham (1894–1973), the aviation pioneer, landed his flying boat at Leith's Western Harbour on Wednesday 6 June 1928 on a stage of his round Britain flight. He was welcomed by thousands of people and a flotilla of boats with sirens sounding.

This seems to have encouraged a local campaign to establish a marine airport at Leith, and in 1929 Leith was approved by the Air Ministry as an airport for flying boats. This never took off as a viable project and it was another twenty years before the idea was revived.

On 1 June 1950, Sir Andrew Murray, Edinburgh's Lord Provost, welcomed the inaugural commercial flight of an Aquila Airways Hythe-class flying boat from Southampton at Leith's new marine airport. The flight from Southampton to Edinburgh took two and a half hours. The flight schedule was intended to be a regular weekly service. The fares were set at £9 single and £16 4s return, which was cheaper than the first-class train sleeper service.

Aquila, which had been established by Barry T. Aikman DFC, was the only commercial operator of flying boats. The twenty-six passengers included Group Captain Donaldson from the Ministry of Civil Aviation, representatives of several shipping companies and some media people. There were seven crew members: Captain A. C. T. Evans, a second officer, an air hostess, two stewards, and engineering and radio officers.

The Aquila Airways flying boat taking off from Southampton on the inaugural flight to Leith Airport.

The plane was moored off the Albert Dock head and a launch brought passengers ashore to be greeted by a welcome party. The plane carried a message from the mayor of Southampton, Dr G. H. Barendt, to Edinburgh's Lord Provost: 'The members of Southampton Town Council join with me in expressing gratification that the Capital city of Scotland and Britain's number one passenger port are now brought closer together, and we hope that the airport at Leith will ever be used for the benefit and service of men of good will.'

It was noted as a 'historic day for Leith' and it was hoped that the new service would 'materially contribute to the transport facilities of those who wanted speedy and comfortable travel'. Unfortunately Aquila Airways had overestimated the demand for the service and within a few months it was declared unviable.

DID YOU KNOW?
Aquila (Latin for eagle) Airways was formed in Southampton in 1948. The company famously ran a flying boat service to Lisbon and Madeira. After a serious accident on the Isle of Wight, in November 1957, the company started to wind down and ceased operations in 1958.

Aquila Airways advert.

25. Leith for Business

There is an air of substantial business-like bustle and activity about Leith's narrow unpretending thorough-fares, and dingy-looking counting houses, which strangely contrasts with the gaudy finery of New-Town trading. The London fopperies of huge plate-glass windows, and sculptured and decorated shop fronts so much in vogue there, are nearly unknown among the burghers of Leith. The dealers are too busy about more important matters to trouble themselves with these new-fangled extravagancies, while their customers are much too knowing to be attracted by any such showy baits. (*Memorials of Edinburgh in the Olden Time*, Daniel Wilson, 1848)

Leith businesses have been at the forefront of innovation and the town is home to a number of distinctive brands.

Rose's Lime Juice

In 1753, it was discovered that a lack of vitamin C was the cause of scurvy among sailors. To prevent this it became a legal requirement for sailors on long voyages to receive a measure of lime or lemon juice, as protection against the disease, giving rise to the nickname 'Limeys' for British sailors. The juice was originally preserved in rum.

In the late 1850s, Lauchlan Rose, the son of a Leith shipbuilder, set up in business as a ship chandler providing provisions for ships. In 1857, he was advertising the supply

Rose's Lime Juice advert.

of West India lime and Messina lemon juice of fine quality in pipes or hogsheads from premises at No. 23 Commercial Place.

Lauchlan experimented with preserving citrus juice in sugar and in December 1867 he received a patent for an improved method of preserving fruit juices. This was the world's first concentrated bottled fruit juice drink – Rose's Lime Juice. It opened up the drink to a far wider market and the addition of a distinctive bottle made it hugely popular. He was awarded further patents for an improved aerated liquid in 1868 and a tool to produce a screw on the neck of a bottle in 1874.

In 1868, Rose set up the first factory to produce the juice on Commercial Street in Leith. In 1893, he purchased plantations in Dominica in the West Indies to ensure his supply and later added a number of other lime plantations in Ghana and the Dominican Republic Gold Coast. In 1957, Schweppes acquired the company and operated it in Leith until 1982.

Crabbie's Ginger Wine

Leith has a long association with whisky. The scores of bonded warehouses in Leith matured a significant amount of the whisky made in Scotland, and Vat 69 was distilled locally by Sandersons. Crabbie's Old Scottish Green Ginger Wine, that essential ingredient of a Whisky Mac, was first created in Leith's Yardheads in 1801 by John Crabbie. Crabbie imported ginger to make the brew from the Far East and the company's distinctive elephant trademark results from the Scottish merchants who pioneered trade with the Orient. The Whisky Mac takes its name from a Colonel Macdonald, who created the drink – equal measures of whisky and Crabbie's green ginger – in the days of the Raj.

Crabbie's Ginger Wine elephant logo.

Pan Drops

The pan drop, a spherical white round mint with a hard shell but chewy middle, has been a favourite confection since it was developed by John Millar & Sons of Leith. The company began in 1844, when Millar started a bakery in Leith that began producing sweets, most famously the pan drop. The firm continues to produce pan drops from a factory in Broxburn.

Drambuie

The well-known legend has it that Drambuie, the honey and herb flavoured liqueur, is based on Bonnie Prince Charlie's secret recipe. The first commercial distribution of Drambuie was in 1910, with the office and production based at the foot of Easter Road. The Drambuie buildings were demolished in the mid-1990s.

Drambuie Building, Easter Road.

Melrose's Tea

The headquarters and warehouse of Melrose's Ltd tea and coffee merchants was at Nos 55–57 Couper Street. Melrose's was a popular brand and they had a number of shops in the Edinburgh area. Andrew Melrose established the company in 1812 and when the tea clipper Isabella landed a consignment of tea at Leith in 1835, Melrose was the first merchant to import tea into Scotland. The Melrose's warehouse, which dates from around 1900, has been converted into flats.

Melrose's Building, Coburg Street.

Crawford's Biscuits

In the firm of William Crawford and Sons, Leith possesses the oldest of the Scottish biscuit manufacturers. It was in 1813 that Mr William Crawford founded the business in a small shop at the Shore of Leith, which, enlarged and modernised, is still occupied by one of his descendants. As every fresh step in the science and art of bread and biscuit making, and every improvement in machinery and method, were welcomed by the founder of the firm, increasing trade quickly outgrew the capacity of the original small premises at the Shore. Modern works were established in Elbe Street. These have been frequently extended and largely rebuilt as the firm progressed, and no trouble or expense has been spared to keep the works equipped with all that is latest and best in machinery and appliances. Crawford's shortbread and Crawford's biscuits have attained a national reputation, and have become widely known in some of the remotest parts of the globe. The factory affords employment to hundreds of Leith men and girls. (*The Story of Leith*, John Russell, 1922)

Crawford's shop on the Shore.

DID YOU KNOW?
The Leith-based William Crawford & Sons made a major contribution to the maxim that Edinburgh was known for the three B's: beer, biscuits and books. The company was founded in 1813. By the 1920s Crawford's employed hundreds of people at their factory in Elbe Street. The girls who worked in factory were known as 'white mice' from the white overalls they wore. The company was taken over by United Biscuits in 1962. Leith's long association with biscuit making ended in 1970 with the closure of the factory.

26. The Buttercup Dairy

Above: The Buttercup Dairy, Easter Road.

Left: The Buttercup Dairy Mural.

The Buttercup Dairy mosaic vestibule at No. 63 Elm Row.

Andrew Ewing (1869–1956), the founder of the Buttercup Dairy Company, was born in 1869 on a farm near the small village of Stoneykirk in the remote south-west of Scotland (a place that is so out of the way that a building in the village was used for a top-secret meeting to discuss the plans for D-Day between Sir Winston Churchill and General Eisenhower). Andrew's father, a tenant farmer, passed away when Andrew was four. The family moved to Stranraer, but in 1882 his mother became seriously ill and there was another move to Dundee to be closer to his mother's parents. Andrew found work in a grocer's shop and by 1894 had his own shop in Dundee. Andrew was ambitious and his first Buttercup Dairy opened in Kirkcaldy in 1904. Within fifteen years the Buttercup was one of the earliest chain stores with 250 branches throughout Scotland.

In 1905, the headquarters of the company was established on Elbe Street in Leith – a strategic move as many of the products sold in the shops were imported from Denmark – and Andrew moved to an address in Montgomery Street. Following rapid expansion, the headquarters moved to larger premises on Constitution Street in 1909, and to an even larger 2-acre site on Easter Road in 1915.

DID YOU KNOW?
The Buttercup shops were famous for their beautiful tiled murals depicting a girl holding a buttercup under the chin of a large, sociable cow. The mosaic vestibule remains at the former Buttercup shop at No. 63 Elm Row.

Ewing purchased Clermiston Mains, a large estate to the west of Edinburgh, and opened an enormous poultry farm that accommodated 200,000 hens. Ewing was a great philanthropist and gave all the eggs laid on a Sunday to local charities. As was his wish, he died close to penniless in 1956, having spent a great part of his life supporting good causes.

27. Jackie Dennis, Leith's Own Rock and Roll Hero

TOP TEN

HERE is this week's list of the ten best-selling records in Britain.* Last week's placings in brackets.

1. MAGIC MOMENTS/CATCH A FALLING STAR (1), Perry Como (RCA). 2. DON'T/I BEG OF YOU (4), Elvis Presley (RCA). 3. NAIROBI (3), Tommy Steele (Decca). 4. THE STORY OF MY LIFE (2), Michael Holliday (Columbia). 5. AT THE HOP (6), Danny and Juniors (HMV). 6. LA DEE DAH (—), Jackie Dennis (Decca). 7. JAILHOUSE ROCK (5), Elvis Presley (RCA). 8. YOU ARE MY DESTINY (7), Paul Anka (Columbia). 9. WHOLE LOTTA WOMAN (—), Marvin Rainwater (MGM). 10. MAYBE BABY (9), Crickets (Vogue-Coral).

*By arrangement with the Melody Maker.

Music chart from March 1958 with Jackie Dennis straight into the charts at No. 6 ahead of Elvis Presley's 'Jailhouse Rock' at No. 7.

The fifteen-year-old Jackie Dennis, Leith's very own rock and roll hero, was bigger than Elvis for a week in 1958 when his first single 'La Dee Dah' was heading to the top of the hit parade, in front of Elvis Presley's 'Jailhouse Rock'. Jackie's record eventually peaked at No. 4.

From the age of eight, Jackie had performed all over Scotland at charity shows. His speciality was vocal impressions of the likes of Al Jolson, Eddie Cantor, Dean Martin and Jerry Lewis. Jackie first performances were in front of his granny at their house in Brunswick Road, where the curtained bed recess was his stage.

Jackie had attended Leith Walk Primary School and Leith Academy, and was working as an apprentice plumber when he was discovered, at the age of fifteen, performing in a show at Prestwick Airport's American air base by Mike and Bernie Winters.

The next week, Jackie got a call and was sent a plane ticket for a trip to London. His auditions for the *6.5 Special*, the top-rated teenage music show of the time, and Decca records were in February 1958. Five weeks later, his first single, the catchy 'La Dee Dah', was in the top ten. Jackie had gone from a £3-a-week Leith plumbing apprentice to a £1,000-a-week teenage rock and roll star.

Right: Jackie Dennis EP cover.

Below: (Left to right) Jackie Dennis, Richard Hayman, Alan King, Perry Como, Anne Jeffreys and Robert Sterling on *The Perry Como Show*, 4 October 1958. (Courtesy of Jackie Dennis)

Jackie's impact was immediate, and he was on his way to showbiz fame and international success. Jackie was quickly added to the cast of the 1958 film *6.5 Special*, along with Petula Clark, Lonnie Donegan, Cleo Laine, John Dankworth, Dickie Valentine, John Barry Seven, Peter Murray and a host of other stars of the time.

Television and live bookings flooded in for Jackie and he was signed for a series of national Summer Shows where he was billed as 'New! Hep! and Fab! The £50,000 Golden Boy from Scotland'. The £50,000 referred to his contract signing fee. His weekly wage was £1,000 and he was the top-billed act, above the likes of Des O'Connor. Jackie released two more records in 1958, 'My Dream', which reached No. 15 in the UK charts, and 'Purple People Eater', which sold 1.3 million copies worldwide and charted at No. 29.

Tommy Steele was one of Jackie's great friends at the time, and Jackie stood in for Tommy after he was mobbed so badly by fans that he had to take two months off from performing. In Germany, Jackie spent time with the Quarrymen, an early incarnation of the Beatles.

DID YOU KNOW?

In October 1958, Jackie Dennis went on to break the United States, many years ahead of the Beatles, when he became the first British artist to appear on Perry Como's Kraft Music Show, which was recorded at the Ziegfeld Theatre in New York. Jackie was on the same bill as the Ray Charles Singers and was introduced as 'Britain's Ricky Nelson'. During his visit to the States to record the Como show, Jackie met the Everly Brothers, and paid a visit to a film set where he was introduced to Burt Lancaster and Kirk Douglas. Jackie also performed with Buddy Holly and Ritchie Valens on the popular music programme *Oh Boy!*

Jackie was proud of his Scottish heritage and almost always wore a kilt or tartan trews on stage. Jackie topped the bill at the Edinburgh Empire (today's Festival Theatre) and starred there in the pantomime *Babes in the Wood* with comedian Jack Radcliffe. At the Sheffield Empire he played Buttons to Petula Clarke's Cinderella and Danny La Rue's Dame.

Jackie's other major achievement was headlining during a four-week residency at the Desert Inn in Las Vegas, where Sammy Davis took him under his wing and he met Dean Martin and Frank Sinatra.

Jackie's one pretension to stardom was a Ford Zodiac with the registration JD 32. Before the days of CDs and even cassettes, Jackie had a record player specially fitted in the car.

After a six-month tour of Australia, Jackie returned to find that Cliff Richard was the new singing sensation on the scene. Jackie continued performing for another ten years in clubs and summer shows, retired completely from show business in the late 1970s and settled permanently back in Edinburgh. Jackie is possibly Scotland's only direct link to the heyday of 1950s rock and roll and a walking encyclopaedia on the subject.